PLANNING FOR

PROPERTY SUCCESS

IN NEW ZEALAND

PLANNING FOR PROPERTY SUCCESS IN NEW ZEALAND

Goal setting and the
six successful strategies

ANDREW KING

RANDOM HOUSE
NEW ZEALAND

National Library of New Zealand Cataloguing-in-Publication Data

King, Andrew (Andrew Martin Duncan)
Planning for property success / Andrew King.
ISBN 1-86941-595-7
1. Real estate investment—New Zealand. 2. Rental housing—
New Zealand. I. Title.
332.63240993—dc 21

A RANDOM HOUSE BOOK
published by
Random House New Zealand
18 Poland Road, Glenfield, Auckland, New Zealand
www.randomhouse.co.nz

First published 2003

ISBN 1 86941 595 7

Cover design: Katy Yiakmis
Printed by Griffin Press, Australia

Contents

Disclaimer

Introduction

Through being deeply involved with property as an investment, I meet many people involved in the industry. I'm often amazed at how little thought many investors give to developing a plan of what they want or require from property and whether their current strategy (if they have one) will in fact take them in the right direction. They usually have a vague idea, but nothing is firmly established. This is a cause for concern, given the large amounts of money involved in any one property transaction. There is a belief that property is a relatively safe investment and, to a certain degree, this is true when compared with many other investment forms. However, property is not without its risks – one of which is losing all your savings and another is that you do not end up with the gains you thought you would.

As a property coach, I first ask my property investor clients what their goals are. This is often met with some confusion, although a typical answer is 10 properties in five or 10 years. For many investors, 10 properties seems to be a magical number – although I have no idea why and, when asked, neither do they. But without a defined and realistic goal, it is difficult to establish what type of property you should be thinking of purchasing, its location, how it should be financed and a timeframe for owning the property.

I often come across the 'wannabe' investor. This is someone who believes that investing in property is a good idea, and wants to invest in property, but somehow just doesn't manage to do so. 'Wannabes' go to many seminars and they talk to lots of people, but they never seem ready to purchase a property. 'I don't know where to start,' they say. I believe that these people have not yet worked out what they want from investment property and are therefore a little bamboozled by the different options available to them – because there are quite a few different options and it can get confusing. The money involved is significant and wannabe investors want to do the right thing. But the trouble is that the right thing for one person may be the wrong thing for another.

This is where good planning comes into its own. A good property investment plan is like a good business plan, in that it is developed specifically for the individual investor, just as a business plan is developed for a specific business. A property plan should take into account the investor's current financial and personal situation, and map out the best way to invest in property to achieve personal and financial goals. It involves considering various options and deciding which will best achieve your goals, given your personal and financial circumstances. This sounds easy, but it is not as straightforward as it sounds and often requires some outside help.

The benefits of good property planning are enormous. It sets things out clearly, giving you more confidence in what you are going to do. It makes it easier to look for property to buy because you focus on certain types and locations. It matches the strategy you decide upon to your own circumstances, which means there is a much better chance of the plan actually working. Planning gives you something to measure results by and helps you make the decisions that keep things on track. By going through a planning process, you are more likely to discover potential risks and develop strategies to overcome them. In short, planning helps you to get started on your investment path and gives you a greater chance of achieving the results that you want. Even experienced investors benefit from planning, as they may not be heading towards the financial results they think they are.

This book provides you with a guide to developing a property investment plan that meets your own requirements. It is centred around analysing your current circumstances in order to establish realistic goals and then achieving them. I suggest some steps you need to consider, and six property investment strategies for investing in property. Not until you complete all these stages, and put all the information together, will you be in a position to develop your own individual plan.

There is no magical blueprint of the best way to invest in property. However, by reading this book I hope you gain the knowledge you require to develop your own blueprint – which will give you a valuable and rewarding document that you can follow towards your own defined success.

If you register on our website at www.PropertyInvestor.Info we will send you updated information on property investment matters, such as changes to regulations, that may affect the information contained in this book.

All the best with your property investments, whatever they may be.

Andrew King

1

Why Invest in Property?

Before setting your goals, it is worthwhile going through some of the main reasons why it can be beneficial to invest in property. One of the key elements I like about property is control. When I invest in property I have total control over what I invest in: how I structure the investment, how I finance the property, how I manage it, how I price it and whether or not I continue to own it. There are also many aspects of property that have benefits over other forms of investment and there are many different ways that you can invest.

Probably the greatest advantage of property is that banks are usually willing to lend you a high proportion of the investment cost, because they view real estate as a relatively safe and stable investment. This willingness to lend money means you can take advantage of leveraging your property investments, which accelerates or multiplies the returns you make. Through the use of leverage, you can obtain very high returns from property, as capital values have tended to rise over time and leverage accelerates these rises. The converse is also true – leverage multiplies any losses you make as well – so it does add a level of risk to your investment. However, as I will explain later, you do not *have* to borrow vast amounts of money to invest in property.

Another good aspect of property is that you can run your property business while maintaining a career, operating another business or raising a family. This gives many people a great deal of comfort, in that they do not feel they are putting all their eggs in one investment basket. But although you may operate your property business as a part-time operation, it still needs to be run professionally. In addition, the amount of time that you have available to invest in property will have a large bearing on what you can achieve. The more time you spend on property, the more you are likely to get out of it.

As property investment is treated as a business, you have access to the various advantages that other businesses have. This includes offsetting income with expenses – including operating expenses (mortgage interest, rates, insurance, etc), home office expenses, and at least part of the cost of running your car.

Another factor that particularly favours investment property is depreciation, which is an allowance by the Inland Revenue Department (IRD) to compensate for the wearing out of any asset (such as machinery, office equipment or vehicles) used to produce income. With investment property, depreciation can be claimed on the building as well as the chattels within the building. Unlike an expense, such as rates, depreciation reduces your tax bill without any money being spent. This has the effect of improving your cashflow.

You cannot claim depreciation on the land portion of the rental property, only on the building and chattels. Property also differs from other assets used to produce income, in that it actually tends to go up in value rather than down. This means that if you sell the property for a profit it is likely that you will have to repay all the tax benefits from the depreciation claims you have made back to the IRD. This is called depreciation clawback. With planning this shouldn't be a problem.

Property investment provides you with two wealth creation streams: rent received and capital gains made. If you decide to live off your investment, your income from property will generally follow inflation, which means that your income and asset base is unlikely to erode over time. This is very comforting to many in their old age and looked on with envy by many who live off the interest from bank deposits.

When your rental properties are well maintained and organised, they are relatively easy to operate. Although there is more effort involved in rental property compared with term deposits or bonds, the returns for your efforts usually make this a worthwhile undertaking, and the effort is not as great as some would make out.

Another potential advantage of investment property is that you do not need to invest any of your own money. If you have sufficient equity in your home or some other asset that the bank can use as collateral, and you purchase a high-yielding property, you may not have to spend anything – and, in fact, you may take income from the property while it increases in value.

There are many different options for you to invest in property – including various types of property, such as flats, apartments and houses; different locations, ranging from suburbs within your own city, other areas in your country to other countries; and many ways to finance property, including the size of deposit (if any), method of repaying the loan (and whether you do), and the type of loan.

Unlike managed funds, management fees are not based on the value of your investment, which can seriously erode your wealth as well as your income. If you employ a property manager, you are paying fees that are a percentage of the rental income rather than the value of the property – and if there is no income from rents, the manager is not paid (again, unlike managed funds, where the manager receives an income whether the fund makes money or not).

Certainly, there are many good reasons to invest in property. But property investment is not for everyone. It involves a level of effort even if you have only one property. It should be regarded as a medium- to long-term investment, which can put people off. There are inherent risks involved with property that make some people uncomfortable. However, I believe that if more people planned their property investment, then they would become more comfortable with the concept and have a far better chance of succeeding.

Planning for property success assumes that you have a reasonable understanding of the basic property investment concepts (as outlined in my first book, *The Complete Guide to Residential Property Investment in New Zealand*), although you may not have bought an investment property yet.

2
Property Planning

Importance of setting goals

Not establishing a plan for your property investment is a bit like not taking a map with you when going on a road trip to somewhere you have never been before. On such a road trip, a map provides you with direction and takes away uncertainty about how you are going to get to your destination. A property plan does the same thing. By establishing a sound plan that takes account of your personal circumstances and potential threats to your investment, you have a much greater chance of arriving at your desired destination.

A good plan is even more important in a low-inflation environment, a situation that has prevailed in New Zealand for some time. During high inflationary periods such as the 1970s, property investors could buy almost anything and it would work out well for them. High-rising property values and rental prices overcame many mistakes investors may have made, so many people did well despite themselves. Since the early 1990s there have been years of very good growth, with an annual growth rate for New Zealand of around 8.5% per annum. Despite a low-inflation environment, house prices continued to do well, especially in the four years up to 1997. However, this may have been because the population were used to, and more accepting of, high-rising property prices. When property prices fell or barely moved in the following four years, it was a wake-up call to many New Zealanders. This situation caused a lot of negative publicity about property and many people became cautious. This atmosphere probably kept prices lower than they should have been at a time when incomes were rising. When high immigration caused an increase in demand for housing, the market took off again. Although the property doomsayers were proved wrong, there is now a more generally accepted view that property prices may not perform as they have done during the 1970s, 1980s and parts of the 1990s.

Annual property price movements

(for years ending 31 March)

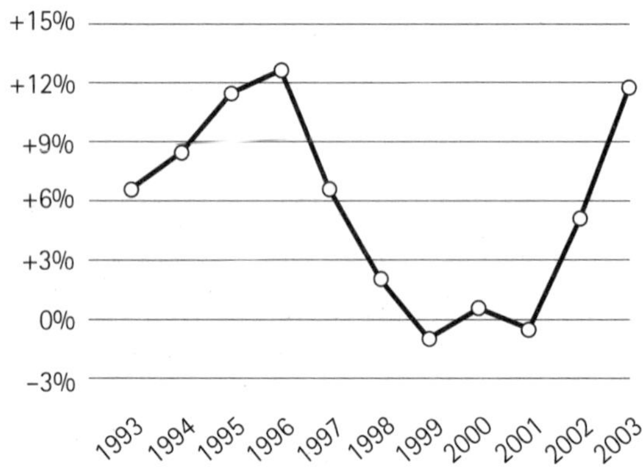

Because of low inflation and people's changing perception of property prices, it is likely that increases will not be as high as they have been in the past. This does not make property a poor investment, because low inflation is also affecting other investment options, including the share market. Companies cannot improve profits through continually increasing prices any more. The lesson for property investors is not to rely on high capital appreciation, which may or may not occur. But this should not put investors off property, because other investments will also be affected and I believe that property will always offer a better return, to the majority of people, compared to managed funds and other similar types of investments.

When an investor assumes or relies on high capital gains, any property will look like a great investment. If you assume lower capital gains, you will be much more selective about what properties you will and will not purchase – this goes a long way towards reducing your risk, and if price rises are higher than expected you will simply reach your goals faster.

Of course, there is not just one property market in New Zealand; rather there are many markets that have their own ways of moving, provide different results for investors and are subject to change for differing reasons. As an example, housing in central Auckland is much more expensive than in Southland. The rental returns are quite different in these two areas, as is the potential for capital gains. Because many new immigrants settle in Auckland, immigration is of prime importance to the area, but has little direct effect in Southland. For these and many other reasons, the central Auckland property market and the Southland property market will provide different investment returns and move in different ways at different times. Either area may be better for certain investors, depending on their individual goals.

Because there are many different ways to invest in property, participants are often confused by choice. A well-devised property plan focuses your attention and establishes why you are investing, what you expect to receive from the investment, how you are going to make it happen and gives a timeframe to keep you on track. With this information, it is far more likely that you will succeed in property and get the benefits you want.

A good goal is a SMART goal

To be workable, any goal needs to be Specific, Measurable, Attainable, Rewarding and Timely. Hence it is a SMART goal. Without such attributes, a goal is really just a vague dream.

When you are setting your property goals, you need to write down exactly what financial performance you require from your investment properties, plus a way of measuring when you have reached your goals and specific steps along the way.

Make sure the goals you set are attainable. You are much more likely to give up if a goal is unrealistic and looms over you as an impossible task. That is not to say that your goals shouldn't challenge you, however. The goals must be agreed or accepted by all members of the household. If your partner doesn't agree to the plan, you need to start over again. The household needs to back the plan 100 per cent.

Remember that it is your goal and no one else's. Other investors may have greater or lesser goals that are entirely appropriate for them and their situations – but this shouldn't mean that you get either discouraged or relaxed about your goals. One person you talk to may be a risk taker who tries to convince you that you need to invest faster and reach higher goals in a shorter timeframe. Another investor may believe your plan is too risky and attempt to modify your goals downwards to meet their own expectations.

While it is good to listen to other points of view, always remember that your goal is for you and as such only needs to be appropriate for you and no one else. If you think others may put you off your goal, then it may be a good idea to keep the goal to yourself. It can be hard enough working towards achieving a goal without having people undermine you by saying you are doing the wrong thing.

One of the most overlooked aspects of establishing a goal is deciding 'why' – 'why am I putting in all this effort to attain this goal?' In other words, what is the reward that you are seeking that makes all the effort worthwhile and keeps you working towards your goal when times get rough. If the reasons you are investing in property are not clear, it is difficult to maintain the effort required to attain your goals.

Focus on income – not on how many properties

When setting goals in property, it is better to decide how much income you want to achieve rather than how many properties. Many investors fall into the trap of saying 'my goal is to own 10 properties' without really knowing why they want that number of properties or what type of properties they are. For instance, buying 10 one-bedroom flats is very different from buying 10 five-bedroom houses – they provide widely different rental prices, costs, yields and improvement opportunities.

Once you have worked out the income you want to generate from your property, you can then establish the approximate value of properties that you will require.

A rough rule of thumb to calculate the value of property you will require is to multiply the desired income by 20. So, if you want a net income of $40,000 per year, the equation would be 40,000 multiplied by 20 – equals $800,000 worth of property. (This assumes a rental yield of around 8%, with running expenses, including a property manager, and tax (including depreciation claims) coming off the gross income figure of $64,000. To achieve the same income figure with property producing a 10% yield, you would need around $660,000 worth of property. The rough multiplier would then be 16.5 rather than 20.)

Desired income	$40,000	$40,000
Rental yield	8%	10%
Rough multiplier	20	16.5
Property value	$800,000	$660,000

Rough multipliers

Rental yield	*multiplier*
5%	28
6%	24.5
7%	22
8%	20
9%	18
10%	16.5
11%	15.5
12%	14.5

The income level that will form your goal should be expressed in today's dollars to take account of inflation. If you don't do this, then you will be underestimating the amount of property that you will require to generate that income.

As an example, you may buy three properties that would

generate around $13,000 each per year without any mortgage. You project that in 20 years' time this income will increase to $30,000 each per year. If your goal is to obtain an income of around $90,000 per year, then in theory you will achieve this in 20 years. However, in 20 years' time $90,000 of income is likely to be worth around $39,000 in today's dollars – that is the $13,000 that each of the three properties is generating today.

If your goal is to have the same spending power that $90,000 will provide in today's terms, then you will need to purchase around seven of these properties – that is, seven multiplied by $13,000 equals $91,000 of income in today's dollars. In 20 years' time this may earn you around $200,000 of actual income; however, this is what you will need to obtain the same spending power that $90,000 will provide today.

As you can tell from the above, the number of properties that you will need to obtain your goal depends on the actual income they will produce plus the rental yield they provide. The higher the yield, the lower the total value of property you require.

Because the type of property you are going to buy hasn't been established yet, you are unable to calculate how many you will need. This doesn't matter at this point, as the actual number is not required, just an estimated income. You will be able to get more detail in your planning when you work out a strategy for achieving the goal you have set yourself.

When will it happen?

After you have determined how much income you need to retire on, you now need to establish a timeframe for when you will achieve this income. This will be your long-term property investment goal.

When establishing when you plan to retire, you should take note of large events that will impact on your life and your property investments. These may include having children, starting a business, undertaking continuing education, moving to a new city or going out to see the world. Your property goals should fit around other goals that you have – and may, in fact, contribute to them.

Case study

When he was 21, Duncan decided he had three goals he wanted to achieve by the time he was 30: buy his own home, graduate with a university diploma in business studies and start an overseas trip of at least two years. His strategy was to continue working as a government employee, while saving for a deposit on a home, which he would purchase when he was 24. Once in his own home, he would begin saving for his overseas trip. He would immediately start studying extramurally for the diploma, which would take seven years and be completed by the time he was 28. He would then spend one year gaining work experience in a position in the private sector and make use of his studies, before leaving on his overseas trip before his 30th birthday. Duncan would rent out his home while overseas and start to invest in more property on his return.

The first part of Duncan's plan was amended slightly when, right on target at 24, he bought two flats, living in one and renting out the other. By purchasing well and fixing up the flats, he was able to increase the achievable rent. One year later, the rental income meant he could finish work and attend university full time, finishing at age 27 instead of 28. He then followed his initial plan of going on his overseas trip before his 30th birthday, but had more time to invest in property and firmly establish himself in his career. He went overseas in a better financial position, which meant he could travel longer. He returned home after three years and was able to purchase a new home and start investing in further rental property.

His plan now is to invest in more property, then sell some to provide capital for a business. He will then concentrate on the business rather than property until the business is firmly established and then return to investing in property again. In addition, he has calculated the possibility of starting a family into his plan.

Why set this property goal?

It is easy to state a specific income that we want to retire on, along with a specific date when we want to attain this income. These are specific and measurable items. But are they rewarding? As discussed earlier, it is good to consider why we have chosen a specific income level as our goal. In itself, money is not a good reward – it is what you do with the money that is the reward. Decide what you want your life to be like when you have a passive income – when you can choose what you want to do with your time unshackled by a requirement to actually spend time *having* to earn money.

You could plan to travel overseas for a specific time period and frequency each year. You could plan to play a sport, spend more time with your family, work for a charity, write poetry, drive expensive cars, or whatever. Once you have determined what you want your lifestyle to be like, you can establish if your planned income will be sufficient, insufficient or excessive in providing it. This process helps you to visualise the rewards you will get through the effort you put into your property investments. It also ensures that when the time comes to live off your investment, you are not going to be disappointed because your income falls short of what you require.

With a desired income and timeframe established, the required value of property calculated and a compelling reason to want to achieve your goal, it is time to work out just what it will take to achieve such a goal.

But before you can take this next step, it is necessary to complete an analysis of yourself and, in particular, your financial situation. This is similar to conducting what is often called a 'business SWOT analysis', which stands for Strengths, Weaknesses, Opportunities and Threats.

3

Analyse Yourself and Your Situation

It is highly unlikely that you will ever achieve a goal that does not take account of who you are and your current situation. The most important feature of this 'personal' analysis is your financial situation. However, you should also consider other more personal factors – such as your attitude to borrowing money, how comfortable you are with risk, your age and your skill base. There are also practical factors to consider, including the time you can devote to your property ventures. Unless these factors are considered and involved in your planning process, you can easily come up with a strategy for investing in property that does not 'fit' well with you, or your partner or family, and this will make achieving your goals much more difficult.

Your financial check-up

Your first task is an inspection of your financial situation.

Your financial check-up should be just like a physical check-up with your doctor. There is little point in ignoring things that are not quite right because you are either embarrassed or don't want to face up to the situation. To be truly useful, a financial check-up should be a frank and honest, if somewhat conservative, analysis of your net worth and how you spend your money. The institution that will lend you the money to buy your properties will ask for this information anyway, so you might as well have it prepared and update it as your situation changes. This not only helps you with planning; it also saves you time when seeking funds for your next property purchase because all the information is available in a suitable format.

Calculating your net worth is simply a matter of adding up all your assets and taking away your liabilities. The figure you are left with is your net worth, an incredibly important figure when applying for funds. Your equity position is another way of saying your net worth, and equity is one of the two things a moneylender will look for when approached for funding. The higher your net worth, or equity, the more you are likely to be able to borrow. Typically, lenders like to see you with 20% equity, or your net worth being 20% of all your assets. The following page contains an example for calculating your own net worth. You can use this form or an electronic version available at www.PropertyInvestor.Info to calculate your own net worth.

Where does the money go?

The second part of your financial check-up is looking at how you spend your money. The key thing is to have a healthy disposable income relative to your total income.

Your disposable income is the amount left over when you take all your expenses away from your total income. If you have a disposable income, it shows that you are living within your means and you have money to put into investments, which can make investing in property much easier.

What you own (assets)	$	What you owe (liabilities)	$
Money at bank/other	25,000	Overdraft	0
Property		Mortgages	
Home	350,000		0
15 Johnston St	285,000	*Bank 1*	210,000
145 Alfred St	620,000	*Bank 2*	545,000
75 Roberts Rd	215,000	*Bank 3*	200,000
Shares	5000	Personal loan	0
Life insurance	0	Credit cards	0
		Limit $7000	
Business value	0		
Vehicles		Other	0
Car 1	4500		
Car 2	8500		
Other	0		
Sub total	1,513,000		
Furniture & personal effects	40,000		
Total assets	1,553,000	Total liabilities	955,000

Total assets	**$1,553,000**
Total liabilities	**$955,000**
Net worth	**$598,000**

You do not have to have a large income to invest in property, but it can certainly help. However, I have clients with six-figure incomes who are going backwards because they spend too much money in all the wrong places. Conversely, I have clients on modest incomes who spend their money wisely and are building up very good investment bases.

No matter what your income level, if you want to start building an investment property portfolio then you need to look at your spending. This doesn't necessarily mean you will have to curtail your lifestyle in any way – but if your existing spending is going to prevent you attaining your investment property goals, then now is the time to find out.

Many of the high-income earners I have met spend a lot of money on such things as cars, boats, houses, entertainment and overseas trips. These are all wonderful things, but if you are spending all your money and time in these areas, you need to be aware that this will have a negative impact on your ability to build an investment property portfolio.

A typical scenario is that of a couple who take out a large mortgage to buy a home then upgrade it a few years later – living with a high mortgage that they can never pay off. At the same time, they are spending their income on disposable items that will not help them build an asset base. Often these people end up with a very pleasant home, nice cars, great furniture, and so on – however, they do not actually own a lot of it and have very little in the way of equity. They would like to invest in property, but the size of their home mortgage severely limits their borrowing potential. Usually they are quite unaware of the situation they are in.

For this reason, it is imperative that you look at where your money is going and form a spending plan to maximise your opportunities. You may decide that you want all the toys and nice things now – which is fine, that's your choice. You may be in a position to be able to afford all the nice things you want – but whatever your income, spending money in these areas is going to limit your opportunities to invest and secure your future with an even greater number of 'nice things'.

The form on the next page can help you to itemise your annual incomings and outgoings, or you can use the electronic version on our website at www.PropertyInvestor.Info or see www.sorted.org.nz. You may need to go through up to a year's worth of bank and credit card statements to identify where your expenditure occurs. A computer spreadsheet greatly helps to develop this information, but pen and paper will lead you to the same result. Note that this form only allows for your personal income and expenditure and you will need to conduct the same exercise for your rental property.

Your strengths and weaknesses

A check on your financial situation is only half the information you require to establish a property plan. The other half is an analysis of yourself. This is essential because you are a critical part of your property investment enterprise. If you think of your investments as a business, then you are going to need a general manager, acquirements and negotiations manager, finance executive, accounts manager, product development manager, maintenance supervisor, customer relations officer and marketing executive. In many instances, these positions are going to be undertaken by you, so you need to know that you have the skills, experience and time to undertake the roles to a high standard.

Household income	**$**
Essential spending	
Housing	
Mortgage or rent	
Maintenance	
Rates	
Insurance (life, health, income protection)	
Utilities (phone, power etc)	
Food & household items	
Clothes	
Insurance	
Doctor/chemist	
Transport	
Petrol	
Maintenance	
Other	
Total	$
Non-essential spending	
Eating out (b/fast, lunch, dinner)	
Takeaways	
Entertainment	
Holidays	
Alcohol	
Cigarettes	
Hobbies	
Other	
Total	$
Total expenditure	**$**
Income less total expenditure equals savings	**$**

You may or may not have the skills, experience or time to undertake many, if any, of these roles. However, you should not let this bother you, because you are still at an analysing stage. Likewise, you should not gloss over the requirements of these positions and just assume that you will be able to accomplish them to a good standard. If you cannot undertake any of the roles, either now or in the future, then it is better to establish that sooner rather than later.

If you are unsure of how to coordinate your property investments, including direction and management to achieve your business goals, then take on the services of a good property coach or establish a relationship with an experienced investor who you can use as a sounding board. Joining your local property investors association (see page 150) is a great way to find good independent advice, whether you have the skills and experience to general manage your property investments or not.

If you do not have the time or interpersonal skills to effectively manage tenancies, then factor a property manager into your planning. If you are not the greatest with figures and bookwork, then get an accountant or bookkeeper to look after the accounts on a monthly basis for you. Although this will cost you more, it will save you a lot of aggravation, time and expense in sorting out mistakes and is a tax-deductible expense.

When conducting this analysis of yourself, you should consider the time you have available to spend on property, your experience and skills, your age and your attitude towards debt and risk. The following expands on each of these points.

Time

Many new investors do not fully appreciate the time that it takes to be a property investor. It is not just the time it takes to manage the property, it is the time spent looking for new acquisitions, the time involved in the sale and purchase process, the time doing accounts, the time needed to maintain the property, the time keeping up to date with industry and economic changes, and so on. In effect, it is a second job – or, more accurately, a second business. As a general rule, the more time you have available, the more you can accomplish with property. If you are planning on a partner performing part of the duties, then make sure they are fully aware of the time commitment and are willing to spend that time to build up a property business.

If you already have a full-time occupation, how much time can you realistically spend on your property investments? When you add family commitments, plus sports and leisure activities and other potential time commitments, what do you have left to devote to property?

It may be that some other activities can be temporarily put aside to give you the time you need for your investment – for instance, you could forgo some leisure activities while proceeding with a property purchase. However, this should be looked at as a temporary measure to resolve a temporary situation.

You should schedule time for activities such as looking in the classifieds for purchasing opportunities (there are more advertisements on some days than others), checking on rental payments, paying expenses, conducting property inspections, routine maintenance or attending property investors association meetings. You should also make sure you have sufficient spare time for handling the spasmodic items that come up from time to time –

things like repairs and getting new tenants, along with more exciting activities such as buying more property.

Time commitments increase with the number of properties you buy; however, the time requirement is not proportional – for instance, it does not take twice as long to manage two properties as it does to manage one. It is a little like having fixed costs and variable costs in a business. You have fixed time commitments for things like looking for property, keeping up to date with industry and economic changes that will not change with each purchase you make. Other time commitments such as checking rental payments, maintaining accounts and paying bills will not double if you increase your properties from one to two – although, of course, they will take up more of your time. By specialising in a particular area and investment strategy, you will become more time efficient as well. Factors that are likely to increase your time commitment proportional to the number of properties you purchase are such activities as finding new tenants and property inspections.

As the number of properties in your portfolio expands, there will come a point when your investment activities become a full-time job, or something near it. At this point, you need to decide whether you will continue with your day job and hire others to perform property investment duties; whether you can work part time and spend more time on your properties; or whether you should quit your day job and become a full-time property investor. This is usually a difficult decision for most people.

The message is that property investment requires time, and there are different strategies that are more or less time efficient. It is important to choose a strategy that matches the time you have available. Your strategy may need to change as you buy more property or when changes in your life alter the amount of time you have to put into your property business.

Skills and experience

We all have different skills and experiences that may make different property strategies more or less appropriate for us. A builder or some other tradesperson or professional in a related field may do very well buying fixer-up or development-type properties – but these may not suit someone without any handy-person skills or decoration flair. Note down all the skills and experience you possess that could have an impact on your property investments, as these are likely to help you in choosing the right strategy.

Age

Property is considered a long-term investment; however, there are strategies that can speed up the wealth-accumulating process. Usually these accelerating strategies involve a higher degree of risk or a greater time commitment. Because there are different options for investing in property, the age of the investor can have a bearing on which strategy is right for them.

Younger people have the benefit of extra years to let property and leverage do its thing – which allows them to let time do much of the wealth generation for them, meaning they can reduce the amount of personal time needed to develop and manage their investment. However, the young may not have the capital or income, or both, to invest in some strategies, so they may be forced into high-involvement, higher-risk property strategies. This can be difficult because young people may also be involved in career development or starting a family and have limited time available to put into their property investment portfolio.

A younger person has the benefit of extra years to correct mistakes or investments that have not gone to plan. Consequently, the young can choose to take on high-involvement or high-risk property strategies with the idea that if things go wrong they will have an opportunity to build their investment back up again.

On the other hand, older investors may not have the required timeframe to use some property strategies and leverage. If there is a short timeframe before a planned retirement date, it may be an insufficient period for some properties to increase in value sufficiently to provide the required income. Because of this, older investors may be forced to undertake higher-involvement strategies in order to build in capital gains so they can reach their property investment goals.

Many older investors may have built up a good deal of capital in their homes over the years and be earning sufficiently high incomes that they do not need to undertake higher-risk strategies. Unfortunately, the short timeframe may mean that older investors are required to downsize their home in order to reach their investment goals, as there is an insufficient timeframe to allow them to use the equity in their home to buy property. In this case you would be physically taking equity from your home and converting it to income-producing equity. As an example, you may have a $600,000 home and $200,000 of investments, meaning 75% of your equity base is in your home and 25% is producing income. You could replace your home with one valued at $400,000, and buy another $200,000 of investment property. By doing this, you now have 50% of your equity actually creating you an income.

The message is to consider your age and when you wish to retire, as this could have a large bearing on the type of strategy you choose for your property investments.

Attitude towards debt and risk

A final factor that will impact on which strategy is right for you is your attitude towards risk and debt. Many people do not mind how much they borrow if they can see that it is taking them towards their goal. For some, however, debt is not so easy to accept and they would not feel comfortable with a large level of debt over their rental properties. Neither attitude is right or wrong – they are simply different. But if you are the type of person who would not sleep at night knowing you owed a large amount of money to a bank, you should take this into account when choosing an investment strategy.

The form of risk known as 'pushing the equity boundaries' is unlikely to be right for the worrier. Banks like to have a 20% equity margin so that if the market falls and they force a sale, the proceeds from the sale are likely to cover the loan amount. Many property investors use the equity in their home as a deposit for investment property, meaning the investment property is 100% financed. If you have a mortgage-free home worth $200,000, then potentially you could borrow all the money necessary to purchase four similar investment properties. The total value of the properties (including your home) is $1 million and the debt is $800,000, so there is a 20% equity level.

	Value $	Mortgage $
Home	200,000	nil
Investment 1	200,000	200,000
Investment 2	200,000	200,000
Investment 3	200,000	200,000
Investment 4	200,000	200,000
	1,000,000	800,000

As long as property prices do not fall, this situation is fine. But if prices fall sufficiently, then the bank could call up all the loans or force a mortgagee sale. If prices fell by 20%, you could lose your previously mortgage-free home.

To remove any risk of this happening, the investor would have to acquire the $40,000 or 20% deposit for each property purchase. Although this doesn't put your home at risk, it is a very cautious and slow way to invest in property. However, this may suit your risk personality and be the right strategy for you.

In between these two options there are a multitude of different ways to invest which will involve a lesser or greater degree of risk. You may be happy to buy one or two properties using your home as equity, then wait for them to rise in value to a point where you are comfortable with the increased equity to borrow and buy more. This could be a 5% increase, 10%, 20% or more. It really depends on your attitude towards risk.

Property investor personality quiz

The following questionnaire is intended to help you identify the kind of investor you are. The results will have an impact on the type of investment strategy that is right for you and how aggressively you pursue it. Challenge yourself to answer the questions honestly and do not be swayed by how you think you should answer. Don't let the opinions of a conservative friend or gung-ho salesperson or investment 'guru' influence you.

1. Are you prepared to do whatever it takes to become a millionaire in:

   A. less than five years B. 5–25 years C. 25 years plus

2. How much are you prepared to pay for coaching or to go to a property investment seminar?

   A. $1500–10,000　　B. $200–1500　　C. less than $200

3. How much of your investment gains would you risk losing through taking on a particular investment strategy?

   A. everything　　B. half　　C. none

4. In order to work towards your investment goal, would you:

   A. use time normally spent with friends, relatives, partners or children to spend more time on property

   B. use time normally spent on relaxing or working around your home to spend more time on property

   C. use time normally spent on unnecessary activities like watching TV to spend more time on property

5. If there were a chance of making more money through a property strategy than you could earn in your current job – but it would require your full-time commitment – would you:

   A. quit working tomorrow

   B. quit if there were a greater than 90% chance of the strategy working

   C. stay with the job as quitting is too risky

6. If you found a property selling for 25% below its true market value, because the seller had lost his/her job and couldn't afford the mortgage, would you

   A. offer 30% below value and consider you were helping the person out

   B. offer 25% below value, feel sorry for the person, but consider that if you don't take the bargain someone else will

   C. offer 20% below value, feel awful about it and often wonder how the person was getting on years later

7. Is your attitude to investment debt:
   A. the more I have the more I am taking advantage of leverage
   B. comfortable with high debt levels as long as I'm covered should interest rates rise by 2 or 3 percentage points
   C. feel uncomfortable with the thought of high debt levels

8. When looking at the financials of a property, you tend to assume that:
   A. good rental and house price growth over the past year will continue for the next year or two and cover the current negative cashflow
   B. some growth should be achievable over the medium to long term
   C. a deal has to stack up the day you buy it as there is no guarantee that the market will ever go up

9. When completing a property deal, would you:
   A. use credit card debt or equity in your parents' house for the deposit
   B. use equity in your home as a deposit
   C. use a saved deposit

10. When negotiating a property deal, would you:
    A. make low offers on many deals at once, reneging if one deal came through
    B. make a low offer on one property
    C. offer the asking price

11. Once you have successfully negotiated a deal, would you:
    A. look for another
    B. slow down looking at property and focus on making sure the current deal is as good as you think it is
    C. worry if you made the right decision and stop looking at other property

12. What do you think it takes to be successful in life?
    - A. high-power get up and go
    - B. good attitude and hard work
    - C. a good education

Mostly As: the audacious investor. You set high goals with a short timeframe and are prepared to do whatever it takes to achieve them. You have no qualms about debt and view a high use of leverage as just a requirement of investment property to enable you to meet your highly challenging goals. You do not allow others' misfortune to influence or hinder you in reaching your targets. You have a nothing-ventured, nothing-gained attitude towards risk, viewing factors that most people would be uncomfortable with as merely a requirement of success. There is virtually no limit on the type of strategy that you will undertake.

Mostly Bs: the adventurous investor. You set challenging yet attainable goals, and are prepared to work hard towards achieving them. You view leverage as a good thing and are comfortable with the high levels of debt that will be necessary to reach your goals. However, you want to be convinced that should conditions turn against you, you have a back-up plan so you will not lose a large proportion of your investment. You do not like to see others in misfortune but can put their situation into perspective and rationalise your actions so that you feel comfortable with them. You have a healthy if guarded attitude towards risk and would probably feel more comfortable knowing that others have successfully accomplished a strategy before you. You would consider most strategies available to property investors; however, you would want a sufficient amount of information before you undertook a strategy you had not tried before and would not rush a decision.

Mostly Cs: the cautious investor. You know how investment property works and you like that it is a relatively safe investment that you have some control over. You do not set high goals because they appear too risky. You can understand the advantages of leverage as you have been to many seminars (except the expensive ones), and have read many books on investment property. Despite this, you still feel uneasy with high debt levels and the risks they bring. You believe that taking advantage of other people is immoral and it would weigh on your conscience if you ever did this. Consequently, bargain properties are not an option for you. You would need to have a high level of confidence that any strategy you undertook would have a high probability, if not certainty, of succeeding.

There is nothing good or bad, right or wrong, with any of these investor types – they are just who you are. Having said that, it is unlikely that a cautious investor will agree with or even condone some of the actions of an audacious investor, who, in turn, would likely view the cautious investor as slow or naïve. This is immaterial, however, as the purpose of the planning exercise is to gain an understanding of the type of investor you are, in the expectation that some of the strategies detailed in chapters 5 to 10 may leap out as being far more suitable to you than others.

If you are going to invest with a partner, then it is also necessary to consider that person's investment personality. You may be an audacious investor, but your partner may be a cautious investor. Remember that neither of you are right or wrong – you simply have a different investment outlook from one another. You need to be aware of this, as it may affect how you invest and can easily lead to conflict.

It is usually better to proceed at the pace of the more cautious investor, and pick up speed when your partner is feeling more comfortable, rather than risk damaging the relationship. In these situations, the more audacious or adventurous investors are often tempted to take control – rationalising this by arguing that their partners are not as interested in the investments and by them taking control, their partners will not have to do things they may be uncomfortable with. This can work well for some factors of investment; however, it comes with the personal risk of putting the more cautious partners under strain. Even if they are not as involved, they are still partners in the business and are affected by the decisions made and the actions undertaken. If they value their relationship, partners will take note of each other's attitudes and respect their comfort zones.

As an aside, note that when you invest in a property with a business partner or relative, banks will treat the entire loan as if it was your responsibility, not just your share of the partnership. As an example, say you own 50% of a rental property with a family member and there is a $100,000 mortgage on the property. Banks will allocate the full debt of $100,000 to you both when looking at any subsequent loan application you make, even when it is on your own. This can have a large and detrimental effect on your individual borrowing capacity.

Many people go to property investment seminars and come out motivated and ready to invest, only to lose this enthusiasm and never put the theory into practice. This is unlikely to be the fault of the presenter – it is more likely the presenter conveyed a plan or strategy that, although it sounded marvellous, did not sit comfortably with the potential investor's investment style or capabilities. So, even on this level, it is crucial that you develop a plan that fits you like a glove – a plan that you feel comfortable with so that you can imagine yourself carrying it out.

4

How to Reach Your Goal

A goal is just a dream unless you have worked out a strategy or action plan for accomplishing or reaching your goal – your goal is your target and your strategy is how you are going to hit your target. Because of this, a strategy is more important than a goal because it is the action or doing part of the equation.

For most strategies that you can undertake with investment property, there is a general concept which many investors follow. This concept is to build up a property portfolio, then at some point sell some of the properties so that the remaining properties are mortgage free. A further refinement of this concept could be to buy high-cashflow properties that would help fund low-cashflow properties with a higher potential for greater capital gains.

For tax efficiency reasons – which make building your portfolio easier – it is best to eliminate any mortgage you have on your home and also any personal debt. This is because personal debt is not tax deductible but rental property debt is.

The capital gains and rental yields for properties in different parts of the country and even in different parts of a city can vary quite widely. A general rule is that property within the centre of a city tends to have higher capital gains and lower rental yields. As you move further out from a city's centre, capital gains tend to fall and rental yields tend to rise. This needs to be considered when you are looking at what area you are going to invest in.

Different types of property have different aspects, such as varying rental yields, and it may be that a particular property type may suit your investment plan better than others. For this reason, it is advisable to consider how particular property types, such as suburban houses, may differ from units, apartments or other property types.

There are a multitude of tactics that investors can take with residential property. I believe that there are just six overall strategies. These six strategies are not mutually exclusive, meaning that you can use two or more of them at the same time with a single property purchase. The six strategies are outlined in this chapter and expanded on in chapters 5 to 10.

Importance of a good strategy

A good strategy is more important than a good goal – because a goal without a strategy is just a dream. You may desire owning a million dollars worth of property, but without working out how you are going to achieve this, it is unlikely it is ever going to happen. The goal gives you something to aim for, but the strategy gives you the blueprint for action.

A strategy can change, however. Chapter 3 looked at you and your circumstances, with the intention of matching these factors with your strategy, but strategies can be fluid and altered to match changing circumstances.

Case study

Jonathon ran a successful business in conjunction with his property investments. His goal was to own $2 million of rental property by the time he was 55 years old, with the intention of retiring and living off the income. His strategy was to purchase property that was likely to increase in value, thereby building an asset base to reach his $2 million target.

At age 47, Jonathon received an extremely good offer for his business, which he felt he couldn't turn down. Selling the business dramatically improved his asset base but reduced his income. Taking note of his change in circumstance, Jonathon changed his focus from capital growth property to high-yielding property so that he could recover most of his lost business income with income from rents.

His plan was still to retire at 55 with $2 million worth of property; however, capital growth was not so important any more.

It is not just personal circumstances that can cause us to change a strategy. Outside factors may also impact on us or provide an opportunity for change.

Case study

Martin owned a block of flats over the road from a technical institute. When the industry for overseas students started to boom, there was a real opportunity to specialise in providing rental accommodation for this growing tenant market.

Overseas students have different requirements for their

accommodation than New Zealand students. Martin put in whiteware so they did not have to find these when they had just arrived in the country, and phone lines into every bedroom so they could connect to the Internet.

By taking these actions Martin was able to increase the rent – which meant he could reach his investment goals faster than before and reduce his exposure to risk factors such as interest rate increases.

Building a property portfolio

The first four of the six strategies I present in this book involve a greater use of leverage, or borrowing money, to enable you to buy more properties than you could without borrowing. Using leverage maximises the potential beneficial effects of rising property prices.

Investors using any or all of these four strategies are likely to use a common concept employed by the vast majority of property investors. This concept is to buy more properties than you actually need to provide your required income goal. The aim is to use leverage to build your equity levels, then, at a predetermined point, sell some of the properties to make the remaining properties mortgage free, maximising your income from these properties. This is a relatively straightforward concept that has worked well for many thousands of investors all over the world. By applying this concept, you can buy all sorts of different properties, use various finance techniques and apply different strategies that will either speed up the timeframe towards achieving your goals or reduce the time that you need to spend on your investments.

The following is an example of how this concept might work.

- ✓ An investor purchases a property in year one for $100,000, using a $20,000 cash deposit, giving 20% equity.
- ✓ Three years later, the property has increased in value by around 15%, so it is now worth $115,000 and the investor has around 30% equity. The investor uses $11,000 saved over the past three years combined with the equity in the first investment property to purchase another similar property for $115,000. So in year three, the investor now has two properties worth $230,000, with $184,000 worth of debt, providing a 20% equity position.
- ✓ Another three years later, prices have again increased by around 15%, so the investor now has $264,000 worth of property with $184,000 worth of debt providing 30% equity. The investor uses another $11,000 of savings and increased equity to buy a third property for $132,000. In year six, the investor now has three properties worth $396,000, with $305,000 worth of debt, providing a 23% equity position.
- ✓ Three years later, prices have again risen 15%, so the investor buys two more properties using the increase in equity and $11,000 in savings. So now, in year nine, the investor has five properties, with around 21% equity.
- ✓ After three years, the investor buys three more properties with the increase in equity and $11,000 in savings. In year 12, the investor has eight properties, with around 21% equity.
- ✓ Three years later, four more properties are bought with the increase in equity and $11,000 in savings. In year 15 the investor has 12 properties, with around 21% equity.

✓ Three years later, the 12 properties have increased in value to be worth $2,777,250 or $231,400 each, with total debt of $1,906,000.

✓ At this stage, the investor sells nine of the properties to pay off all the loans, and retains three properties debt free with a cash surplus of over $100,000 after selling costs.

Example of building a property portfolio

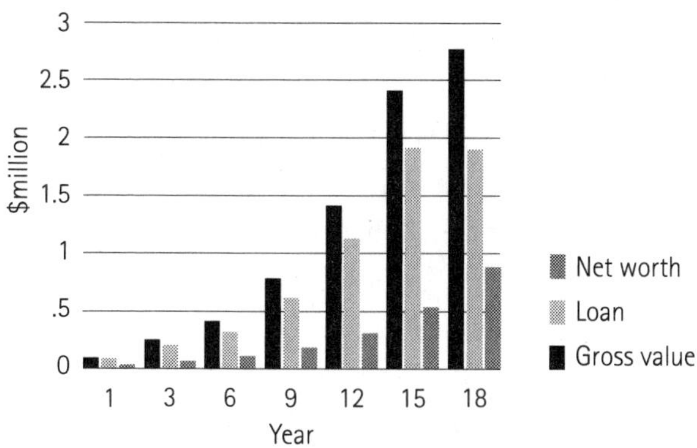

Pay off your own home first

If you have a mortgage-free home, this will undoubtedly help you to invest in property, although it is not essential. If you do have a personal mortgage or debt, then it is best to transfer it into investment property debt wherever possible. This is because the mortgage interest on your home is not tax deductible but the interest on your rental property mortgage is.

From a tax perspective, it is far better to have tax deductible debt than non-tax deductible debt. This means that you should take any opportunity to reduce your home mortgage or any personal debt before reducing rental property debt. If you have a home mortgage plus $40,000 in cash and want to buy an investment property, use the cash to reduce your home mortgage rather than as a deposit on the rental property. You can use the equity in your home as the deposit and borrow all the funds necessary to buy the rental property. Even if this means you need to top up the cashflow for your rental property, you will still be better off through the reduction in your home mortgage payments.

If you limit the size of your home mortgage, then you will also pay it off faster. Paying the mortgage off fast means you will have more money to spend on luxury items or, preferably, more money to invest in rental property or other investments.

The key point is that the more equity you have in your own home – either through increasing market value or paying off personal debt, or a combination of the two – the more investment property you can buy. You can use the equity in your home as a deposit, rather than any savings you may have, and borrow the entire purchase price. This frees your savings to be used for personal debt reduction.

Strategic locations

The areas that traditionally provide a low rental yield but high capital gain are centrally located, have a high socioeconomic profile and are near water or with water views or some other favourable aspect. Typically, there is a combination of high demand and a shortage of available land for new developments in these areas, so the law of supply and demand tends to push up values. However, just because a property is located in such an area does not mean you cannot obtain a good rental yield from it. It will usually require some extra work, such as renovating, developing or changing the use of the property.

Properties that generally produce high rental yields tend to be located in outer suburbs and lower socioeconomic areas. Although these areas usually have high rental yields, they also have higher management problems and higher rent arrears, which should be taken into consideration with your planning.

High-yielding properties do provide capital gains as well, even if they are not as high as other areas. Capital gains can also be built into these properties by fixing them up or developing them. Properties in locations that often provide high rental yields may also have large sections, which may be developed or used in some other way to increase the value of the property or the achievable rent.

Although the location of the property is important, it may change over time. This is because a country's housing and rental market is made up of many smaller markets, each of which goes through cycles – and it is unusual for them to be at the same stage of a cycle at the same time. This may mean that an area that once provided high yields may change over time so that high-yielding property is difficult to find. This often happens when an area becomes highly desirable. Owner-occupiers are often prepared to pay high prices to live in these desirable areas. Although this often also causes a rise in rental prices, the increase is usually not as great.

Different property types

The two main types of property in New Zealand are houses and units. (Although the number of apartments has certainly increased in the last 10 years, they still make up a small proportion of properties in New Zealand.) It is generally thought that houses provide better capital growth than units; however, this is not always the case. The following is a brief summary of the different property types commonly available in New Zealand and how they can fit into your plan.

Houses

Houses can either be on their own site or on a cross-lease site. Houses are stand-alone dwellings and are generally preferred to units by the majority of tenants and owner-occupiers – because usually they are more private, larger and have more outdoor space (note: this generalisation does not apply to all population groups who may prefer other types of dwellings).

In any given area, houses may be worth 20% to 40% more than units with the same number of bedrooms, yet the achievable rent is only 5% to 20% greater. This means that houses tend to produce a lower yield than units because the comparative increase in their achievable rent is less than the increase in their capital value.

Houses have advantages over units in that they often have unused land that can add both rental and capital value. For instance, you can add a garage, carport, sleepout or even subdivide a house on its own section – all of which are difficult to achieve with a unit. Houses on cross-lease sections offer fewer opportunities for adding value because their sections are generally smaller – although, typically, there is still more chance to add value with a house on a cross-lease section than there is with a unit.

Houses may also suit certain tenants better than others – for example, families tend to like houses that have outdoor areas for children to play in.

Units

Units can either be on separate titles or multi-units on one title. Units on separate titles tend to be more valuable than multiple units on single titles because they are more flexible – you can sell one or more units in a block separately if they are on separate titles. Separate title units may also appeal to owner-occupiers, whereas multiple units on single titles tend to be bought by investors only.

It is a widely held belief that units do not increase in value at the same rate as houses. This is based on the idea that increases in value are due to the land rather than the building, and there is usually little land with a unit. But a study of property price rises in New Zealand's main urban areas over the seven years from March 1995 to March 2002 showed that there was very little percentage difference in unit and house prices changes. (Note that the dollar value difference did increase, however, as houses started from a higher base rate.) The graph on the next page shows a very similar trend for both houses and units over this period.

Units have some advantages over houses in that they are generally more robustly constructed and easier to maintain. When they are getting older and tired, it is relatively easy to spruce them up and make them look appealing again, and thus maximise achievable rental prices.

As mentioned previously, units also provide a higher yield than houses, so they tend to be easier to fund. The downside of units is

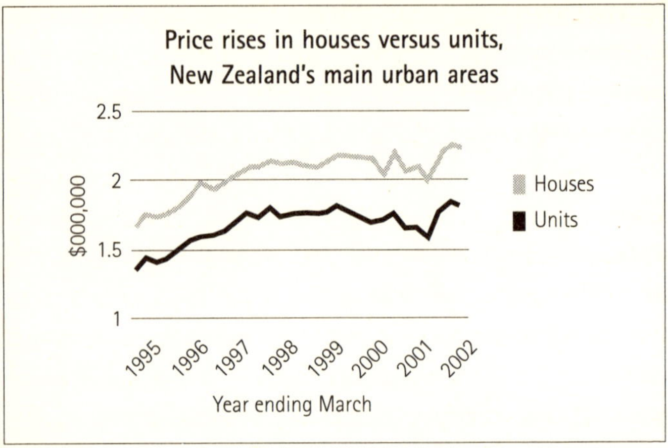

that there are limited opportunities to add value to them because they are usually sited on small sections. Of course, you can buy distressed units and fix them up. However, with units you tend to just receive natural increases in market value rather than self-generated increases in value.

Townhouses

Townhouses are up-market units, or terrace houses. They are usually more modern, more spacious and have more features than units – for example, an internal double garage and a fitted kitchen.

Townhouses are more expensive than units, but tend to achieve the same rental yield as houses without the ability to add value (because of small sites). They offer limited value-added opportunities and lower rental yields than units, and therefore tend to be owned by owner-occupiers rather than investors.

However, as investments they do have the advantage of tending to attract good tenants – because of their modern and above-average features – which helps reduce management time.

Apartments

Apartments are a popular form of housing overseas, where cities are larger and space is at a premium; however, they have only been built in significant numbers in New Zealand since the early 1990s.

Different apartments are designed for different purposes. Those designed for the owner-occupier market tend to be spacious and well appointed but achieve low rental yields. There are some that are constructed for the rental market and these provide a good gross yield; however, body corporate fees *(fees paid to a group who administer the complex and handle items such as maintenance and insurance)* can reduce the bottom line considerably.

Some of the rental apartments, particularly those specifically aimed at the student market, are very small, and if the overseas student industry falters it is doubtful that regular New Zealand tenants would want to live in such apartments. These small apartments can be extremely difficult to fund due to lenders not being comfortable with their small size.

There are also apartments designed as hotel rooms, which are usually leased back to a hotel chain or management company. The success of these investments depends upon the health of the tourism industry and how well the hotel or management company market the rooms. Investors are tempted by guaranteed rental incomes; however, many rental prices have fallen – some by as much as half – when the rental guarantee period expires.

As with townhouses, there is little that you can do to an apartment to pro-actively increase its value, so you tend to be subject to natural market forces to increase their value. Lending institutions are reluctant to lend on the same favourable terms that they provide for houses and units, so investors in apartments usually have to have a large equity base to work from.

Holiday homes

Holiday homes are becoming a popular investment option due to the increase in prices of coastal properties and the fact that investors can use the properties when they are not rented out.

Holiday homes that are run as a business have the same tax conditions as ordinary rental property. This means that expenses can be claimed as long as the property is available for rent. However, if the owner has marked off set periods throughout the year for personal use of the property, then expenses cannot be claimed for these periods.

Depreciation rules are the same for ordinary rental property; depreciation on chattels is especially advantageous for holiday homes, which are usually furnished and may also include recreational equipment.

Marketing and administration are two key areas that make this type of investment a more hands-on business. Good marketing is essential, as are good systems to take bookings, organise keys, check on cleanliness, and so on.

For more information on holiday homes, see Mark Withers's book, *Property Tax in New Zealand* (available for $24.95 from Withers Tsang & Co Ltd, www.wt.co.nz).

Six key property investment strategies

Although there are many different types of property that you can invest in, I believe there are only six main strategies for investing in rental property (although some would say that there are many more than six). Within these six strategies, there are a great many options. I have not included holiday homes, houses, units, apartments and other property types as different strategies, because each of these property classes can fit into all of the six key strategies.

The six strategies are:

1. ordinary properties
2. bargain buys
3. fixer-uppers
4. developments
5. buy and pay off the loan
6. living off excess cashflow.

In the following six chapters, I will explain each of the six strategies for investing in property. These strategies are for property investment rather than property speculation. Property investment is buying property for its rental return and longer-term capital growth. Property speculation is buying or developing a property with the intention of selling it for a profit in the short term.

The six strategies are not mutually exclusive, meaning that a combination of strategies can be applied to a single property. You can buy a bargain that also lends itself to development and fixing up for even greater profits.

None of the strategies is right or wrong, better or worse, than any of the others. They each have good and bad points and are more suitable for some investors as opposed to others. It is important to be aware of the strategies so you can focus your efforts on the one or two that best suit you and fit in with your circumstances and goals. By specialising on one or two strategies, you will become more expert at them and have a greater ability to maximise your return. You will also save time looking for property because you can focus on properties that fit into your criteria.

5

Ordinary Property

Buying an ordinary property does not sound very exciting. However, there are some good reasons why this may be a suitable investment strategy. Buying an ordinary property, regardless of its location, means buying a property that is perfect as a rental property straight away without any (or very little) further work being necessary. It does not necessarily mean the property is immaculate, but it does mean that it has all the features usually required by the tenant target market in that area. For instance, if it is intended for a family, the property will be fenced with enough section for children to play in, plus have a driveway and garage, the kitchen will be well appointed and there will be a bath in the bathroom.

The property will require no – or minimal – initial maintenance, and will be ready to let on the day it is purchased. Likewise, there is no ability for further development of the property to increase its value.

Under this strategy, you are unlikely to get the property at a bargain price because it will have wide appeal to a large number of potential homebuyers as well as investors. Essentially, there will be nothing to put potential buyers off. The location is unlikely to cause any potential problems. It may be near shopping centres, transport or work areas, schools, cafés or learning institutions – whatever facilities are required by the potential tenant target market.

This type of property could be a new or near-new home, or an older property that has been well maintained. New properties offer an advantage over older properties in that the depreciation claims tend to be higher because the chattels make up a higher proportion of the overall value of the property.

As an investor, you would pay market or near-market value for the property and would likely find a tenant willing to pay a market rental price. As such, the property would provide a reasonable or average rental return. As there is no work to be done on the place or development opportunities, any capital gain the property may make is entirely determined by the market.

Advantages

The benefit of this type of property is that there are thousands of them available for sale in the newspapers and in real estate agencies every day. Although ordinary property is popular with a wide variety of people, owner-occupiers are often very selective about their next new home, so you may have less competition to purchase the property than you may think. Because these properties are easy to find and easy to purchase, the investor does not have to spend as much time searching for investment property.

Ordinary property is easy to let because it already has the features that tenants want in a property in that location. This saves the investor time by not having to install any features before the property can be let. As there are no maintenance issues, the investor doesn't lose time organising tradespeople or doing maintenance before the property can be let.

Because the property is ready to let the day you take possession, there is no down time. The property starts earning its way from day one.

If the property is new, then the proportion of chattels and fit-out in proportion to the rest of the building will be high. This means that you can gain a higher tax deduction through higher depreciation claims. This, in turn, will lead to a better cashflow situation, in the first few years at least, while the book value of the chattels are still high.

You can easily establish that this property will be a good rental and what rental price it will achieve, based on rents achieved by similar properties in the same area. There is no guesswork because what you see is what you get. This makes planning easier.

Property managers prefer this type of property and thus will be more than happy to take you on as a client. This means you can pick the best property manager for the area.

Disadvantages

Ordinary properties only provide ordinary returns. There are no opportunities to add value to the property and achieve capital gains or rental price increases other than natural market appreciation over time. This can mean that it takes longer to reach your property investment goals.

If there is a downturn in the market, nothing can be actively enhanced to counter the negative movement. You have little control on how the property will perform. The effect of a rental or property price reduction introduces an element of risk. If rental prices fall, or interest rates rise, and you can no longer afford to service the mortgage and other expenses, you may be forced to sell the property. If the value of the property falls significantly, the bank may feel you have too little equity and call in the loan, forcing you to sell.

With no opportunity for large initial increases in equity, it is far more likely that you will need to save the deposit for subsequent property purchases, rather than using the increased equity in the existing property. This makes it harder to purchase further properties. If rental and property prices fall, then it will be even harder to purchase more property at a time when there may be good bargains available in the market.

Ordinary properties often provide a rental return that does not cover all outgoing expenses. This means that to ensure cashflow commitments are met, you either need to have a large cash deposit (to minimise borrowings and interest payments) or surplus income with which to service any shortfall in rents to cover expenses.

Investor match

Ordinary properties suit investors who have limited time to put into their investments. This may be people who have busy careers, or high time commitments involving such things as business, family or sport.

Ordinary properties suit high-income investors who do not require large rental returns from time- and energy-demanding property investments. They are a great place to invest your money long term to reap the benefits of an upward property market and the positive effects of leverage.

Although there are other property strategies that provide larger returns, ordinary properties can still perform well compared with other investment classes. High-income investors can purchase another property whenever they have saved a sufficient amount for a deposit. This becomes easier over time as equity builds up in their existing properties, and they use this equity to help fund subsequent purchases.

For similar reasons, investors with high cash reserves can suit ordinary property. By using their cash as a deposit, they can reduce the size of the required mortgage so that the rental return is sufficient to make the property cashflow neutral or even provide an income.

If ordinary properties are bought in locations where there is a good chance for high capital growth, then a negative cashflow can easily be outweighed by capital gains. Negatively geared properties also present good tax deductions, which can favour investors on high marginal tax rates, as these investors obtain a better tax refund than investors on lower tax rates.

Young investors can benefit from ordinary properties as they have time to let the investments reach their potential, and the time to build their portfolios at a slower rate. A potential disadvantage for younger investors is that their income is often insufficient to save for the deposit or carry the negative cashflow.

In addition, ordinary properties suit those investors who do not have the skills, experience or inclination to want to fix up or develop properties.

Risk-averse people like ordinary property because what you see is what you get – making them easier to analyse with a high degree of accuracy.

Overview of ordinary properties

Advantages

- Easy to find and purchase.
- Easy to predict how they will perform in the short term.
- Saves time and effort.

Disadvantages

- May not increase in value sufficiently or quickly enough to reach your goals.
- Lack of control (passive use of market forces).
- Harder to buy successive properties.
- May need higher deposits to maintain adequate cashflow.
- May require regular cash inputs to maintain adequate cashflow.
- If the property market falls soon after purchase, your equity position may fall below 20% and the bank may call in the loan.
- If the rental market falls soon after purchase, you may have insufficient income to meet expenses.

What investors suit an ordinary property?

- High-income earners.
- Those with large cash reserves.
- Those with little spare time.
- Young people with longer investment timeframes.
- DIY-challenged investors.
- Cautious investors.

Example of an ordinary property

Property	$200,000
Deposit	$40,000
Rent (yield 7%)	$270 pw
Property manager at 7.5% of rental income and Interest Only loan	
Value of property after 10 years	$256,017
Equity after 10 years	37.5%
Return if sold after 10 years	$73,084
Excess rental income over 10 years	$6605
Cumulative annual return on investment	7.1% (average 9.9%)

Assumes 2.5% inflation rate; house and rental prices plus expenses increase by the inflation rate; mortgage interest rate of 7.5%; building depreciation clawed back; 50% of chattel depreciation clawed back; real estate agent fees.

Case study

I bought a house in central Hamilton in 1989 for $68,000. It was a four-bedroom house in average order, which I thought would be ideal for students. The rental was $195.00 per week, which provided a gross yield of 15%. Although this sounds high in today's terms, in 1989 this was an average return because interest rates were also 15% at the time.

I put down a 20% cash deposit and borrowed the remaining $54,000. After principal plus interest mortgage payments, management fees and other expenses, I needed to put in extra money to keep the property afloat. This situation remained for the first two years; however, interest rates then dropped to 10% and the property became cashflow positive.

After 14 years, the property is now worth $150,000, which is a compounded increase of around 6% per year. Rental price increases have not kept pace with house price increases over that time. The weekly rent is now $250, which is a little under 2% compounded growth per year. This has had the effect of reducing the rental yield to around 8.5%, which interestingly is about average for the area.

Although I made principal plus interest mortgage payments, even if I had maintained the $54,000 original loan, my return on the original $14,000 I invested was $82,000 or an average return of 41% per year. This would not include any of the excess income earned from rent.

Pieter Geill
Wellington

6

Bargain Buys

Bargain properties are simply a good buy – a property that you have bought for less than its true market value or one that can provide a higher rental return. These properties are more difficult to find than ordinary properties, because everyone wants a bargain and nobody wants to sell for less than something is worth. Because of this, it takes up more of your time to locate bargain properties and you may have to act quickly when you find one.

When selling a property, all manner of statistics can be gathered that can help to gauge the value of a property. However, even when armed with factual information, other factors come into play that can affect the actual price achieved. There are reasons why a seller may want to sell the property quickly and is willing to accept a lower price so the sales process will be as fast as possible. He or she may also be willing to accept a lower price if the offer is very 'clean'. By this I mean that the buyer makes an offer that includes no or very few conditions, can go unconditional quickly, and can settle in a short or long timeframe that suits the seller's circumstances.

On the buyer's side, homeowners buy property for emotional reasons as well as financial ones. Two properties that have essentially the same features and are in the same condition and location can still attract different interest from homebuyers because one property has a certain 'something' that the other doesn't. From an investor's point of view, it is likely that the achievable rental price for these properties will be the same, meaning that the less desirable property will provide a better rental yield. However, do not be fooled into thinking that it is worth the same as the other property in its present state – unless whatever is turning people off the property is identified and fixed, this property will never achieve the same value as the first property. But it is likely that the values of the two properties will increase at the same rate, and the higher-yielding property will be easier to fund over time, making it a bargain of sorts.

Finding bargains

There are three classic reasons – called 'the three Ds' – why sellers may be willing to sell a property at a bargain price: death, divorce and de bank. In addition, there are at least three other reasons why properties may be bargains: desperate vendors, vendors who do not know the true value of the property, and properties that are poorly marketed.

Death

At the time of a bereavement, there is the likelihood that a property will be passed on to descendants, often the children of the deceased. In this situation, the beneficiaries of the estate often want to sell the property quickly so that the proceeds can be dispersed among themselves. It can be an unpleasant task to sell the home of a loved one and beneficiaries usually want the process handled as quickly and easily as possible. It is also difficult for groups to make a decision on what price to sell for and, when faced with a share of the proceeds, many look at what they are personally giving up to achieve a nice quick sale. As an example, if the proceeds of the property are to be divided among 10 relatives, then receiving $5000 less than what they want for the property works out at only $500 each, minus commission. This makes the individual's decision to sell a lot easier. In addition, beneficiaries often feel that they are not actually giving anything up by accepting a lower offer than they thought they might achieve. Whatever they receive can be viewed as a blessing, which is a different mindset from when you are selling your own property that you have paid for yourself and likely funded through a mortgage.

For these reasons, people who are inheriting a property can be willing to accept a lower price than an owner-seller. To be in a position to meet these people's requirements, investors should be well organised. This means having deposit and finance in place, plus a good knowledge of the area so that you can make a quick decision and accommodate whatever the beneficiaries want.

Divorce

Divorce is another unpleasant occurrence that can lead people to accept a lower price in return for an easy exit from a difficult situation. A word of caution, though – these negotiations can be drawn out and tough because the two parties often do not cooperate with each other. Emotions are high and one or both parties can make seemingly irrational decisions for reasons that you may never know. The whole process can even be brought to an abrupt halt if one of the parties decides to stay on in the property.

There is a real need to at least try and understand what the parties are going through and attempt to meet their needs in order to obtain a good purchase price. This may involve some creative thinking on your part, such as buying the property but allowing one party to stay on as a tenant while he or she sorts out what to do. An accommodating approach like this can help them through a difficult period in their lives while providing you with a bargain property deal.

Mortgagee auctions

The third 'D', de bank, occurs when someone is having financial problems and cannot keep up with mortgage repayments. The bank has decided to repossess and sell the property to reclaim the money that is owed to them – this is usually called a mortgagee sale. Under these circumstances, a bank is really only interested in receiving the outstanding debt and costs involved in handling the sale, which means that a bargain price could be achievable. Although a mortgagee auction operates in a similar way to a regular auction, there are some points to be wary of and it is wise to seek legal advice before you purchase.

One catch is that there is no right to object to any defects in the title. Cross-lease properties present a good example of this. In a normal sale and purchase agreement, if a buyer found that an extension to the dwelling was not shown on the cross-lease title, then this would be a reason to withdraw from the sale. But, with a mortgagee auction, the buyer would not be able to do this. Because of this, your lawyer should check the title before you attend the auction. The same goes for a LIM report. The standard sale and purchase agreement contains a LIM condition, but this is not included in the conditions of a mortgagee auction. Therefore, you should obtain a LIM, or if you do not have time, an inspection of the local council's property files, to see if they contain any concerns that the council is aware of. The following are some further points to consider.

You need to check whether or not the property is sold with vacant possession or 'as is, where is'. At some mortgagee auctions, the property will be sold on the basis that the purchaser is obliged to remove the occupant. In most cases, previous owners will often leave without any fuss. However, they may feel aggrieved at their situation and refuse to leave, even if this is unlawful. In such a situation, the purchaser has no power to go into the property and take possession – if you did this, you may find yourself being prosecuted by the police. The only way to legally remove an unlawful previous owner is to apply to the courts for a writ of possession (note that the Tenancy Tribunal does not apply in this case). This may be an expensive and time-consuming process, and legal costs and loss of rent while the matter is sorted out could see you lose $10,000 or more.

Another potential problem is caveats, which are written notices of another party's interest in the property. Caveats usually cover a lender's interest in the property and are set aside under a mortgagee auction. However, mortgagee sales often involve rent to buy or similar schemes where there is a long-term sale process. The original seller, in this instance, is likely to record his or her interest in the property – and a caveat lodged by a long-term purchaser can only be set aside by a court order. Some banks include a clause in the mortgagee sale conditions that if this occurs and the bank cannot release the caveat, then it will have no obligation to do so – making it, in effect, the purchaser's problem. This could be a serious difficulty for any purchaser. Hence, it is essential to check for any caveats against the title and, if there are, that they relate entirely to lending.

The auction agreement will not usually include a right for a pre-settlement inspection. This can make it difficult to see what potential problems you are buying, especially if an aggrieved and unhelpful owner refuses you access. If the property is unoccupied, then the agent will be able to show you through. However, if there is an aggrieved occupant, then the risk of damage being done to the property is particularly high. In addition, the chattels do not form part of the property, and could be taken away by the previous owner. As most property investors know, the items that can constitute a chattel can be wide and varied and make a significant impact on the value of the property and the length of time it takes to get the property ready to let.

The disadvantage of the mortgagee sale is that you cannot cover yourself for all the potentially negative outcomes, and you have no way of knowing whether or not they will occur. This increases the risk factors that you should consider and allow for when considering purchasing property through a mortgagee auction. If everything goes well, then it is likely you can get a bargain; however, the safety margin you allow could easily be eliminated should something (or everything) go wrong.

Mortgagee auctions are often advertised in newspapers under the usual 'property for sale' section. They are noticeable, as the photos tend to be in black and white rather than colour. A quick check with the agent will usually let you know whether it is worth pursuing as a rental property or not.

Uninformed vendors

These are people who, for one reason or another, do not know the value of their property or genuinely believe that the property's value is less than it really is. Private sales are becoming a good source for bargain buys. There seem to be two sorts of private sale situations. The first is that the seller has an inflated idea of what the property is worth and tries to maximise his or her return by attempting to eliminate the agent's fee. The second type is unaware of what the property is worth and sells it too cheaply – possibly because they think they should take off the agent's commission from the price they think they will get. Many people are unwilling to buy privately because they do not like negotiating directly with the owner, so the potential number of buyers in competition with you to obtain the property can also be reduced.

Unsuccessful landlords can also be a good source of property bargains. Often they have not kept rents up to date with market levels, have selected tenants poorly and mismanaged the property. They cannot believe that anyone would want the property after they have had so many problems with it and offer it for sale based on a low rent and high management costs.

Poorly marketed property

This opportunity is closely related to uninformed vendors. Poorly performing real estate agents may have little idea of what a property is worth, have little or no negotiating skills or apply what they would pay for the property as an asking price, rather than what the property is really worth. The promotion may be poor, which means that few people know the property is for sale. The agent offers little advice to the vendor on how to present the property to its full advantage and has little awareness of the key selling features of the property so does not instil eagerness in those potential buyers who do manage to view the property.

The property tends to sit for a while, which also puts some people off as they think there is something wrong with it, or has some fault that they haven't considered but others have. This all amounts to a potential advantage to the property investor.

Desperate vendors

Desperate vendors are similar to vendors who have inherited property or are selling the family home because of a divorce situation. The only difference is that they may not be in a negative situation.

Vendors who have bought their next home before selling their old one can be desperate to sell and move on. These vendors often have little time to sell their property, and are usually so emotionally attached and unwilling to lose the new home that they are willing to take a lower-than-market-value price for their old home. The use of cash-out clauses can also turn calm vendors into desperate vendors, when faced with having to go unconditional within five days or lose their new home. If they go unconditional, they will usually be forced to sell their old home quickly.

Other vendors who have bought a new home before selling their old one use bridging finance, effectively owning two homes and most of the expenses this involves. When the mortgage payments and bills start to mount up, these vendors soon realise that they may have been optimistic about the selling timeframe and be willing to accept lower offers for a quick sale.

Case study

Owners of an Auckland subdividable property turned down a $650,000 unconditional offer from a developer to purchase the property. The property continued to be marketed without a price but did not sell. The owners had already bought a new home and used bridging finance to settle. They moved out of their first home.

A few months went by and the property did not sell, with many potential buyers believing the vendors wanted too much for the property. The property eventually sold to another developer for $570,000, which was a considerable saving on the true market value.

With little enhancement to the property, the developer put it back on the market a few months later and sold it at auction for $740,000.

Advantages

The key benefits of buying a bargain are that you lock in extra equity from day one and you provide a risk buffer in case the market changes adversely.

By buying a property that is undervalued, you immediately add equity and the opportunity to refinance in, say, six months' time. If the value of the saving is sufficient, this may mean freeing up your deposit to use for your next property, or not having to use other property to provide security for the bank. With either your deposit or your equity in other property returned, you are then in a position to use it again to buy more property.

Having built-in equity also means you are not a passive investor going where the market takes you. Even if the market remains static, you have still moved yourself closer to achieving your goals.

Should you purchase five properties for 20% under market value, then you effectively own one of these properties outright, and it would only take a property price increase of around 5% for you to be able to sell four of these properties to cover selling costs and own the fifth outright. If they were ordinary properties, the market would have to increase around 25% for you to be able to accomplish the same outcome.

Bargain buys provide a degree of risk elimination through acting as a buffer to downturns in the market. By providing either instant capital gains or rental increases, you protect yourself should either the housing market or the rental market, or both, take a fall. This type of protection is especially useful at the top of any property cycle when the chances of a market downturn are highest.

Through purchasing bargain properties you are likely to achieve your investment goals at a faster rate than if you bought ordinary properties.

Disadvantages

Because there are fewer bargain opportunities and everyone wants a bargain, these types of properties are generally harder to find compared with ordinary properties. The time it takes to find these bargains should not be underestimated. Many investors get frustrated because they cannot locate these properties as easily as they would like and, consequently, lower their buying requirements to make it easier. This is not advisable.

When buying a bargain you are often buying at someone else's expense and this makes some people feel uncomfortable. Others take the view that you are helping the vendor out of an unfavourable situation, or if they didn't take the opportunity someone else would. Some people feel sorry for the vendors, leading them to believe they are taking advantage of their misfortune, which they find unpleasant and even immoral. If you believe this, then buying bargains may not be the strategy for you.

A third downside is that there may be a very good reason why the property is available for a bargain price and it is, in fact, not a bargain at all. There is a higher risk element when buying bargain properties because of this, so it pays to do your homework.

If you make use of the increased equity to borrow more money on the property, then you do not have as high a margin should property prices drop in the short term. This could leave you exposed to the bank calling in the loan and potentially being forced to sell.

Investor match

Bargain properties suit investors who have the necessary time to seek out these types of property, as it can be a very time-consuming activity. There is a saying that you will need to look at 100 properties, make an offer on 10 and negotiate on three just to get one bargain. When the market is strong it can take even longer. Bargain hunters need to have a lot of time available to regularly look at property advertisements, contact their team of real estate agents and conduct other activities such as door knocking to try and find their next bargain. If you do not have the time to do this, seeking bargain properties may not be the ideal strategy for you.

Bargain properties suit pragmatic people who understand that unwelcome situations can fall upon people and may force them to sell a property at lower-than-market value. Bargain hunters cannot afford to let the unfortunate situation of the vendor hinder them in obtaining a bargain, yet some sensitivity can help with negotiations and even provide a better outcome for all parties. You do not need to be a ruthless person; however, you do need to appreciate that the vendor's situation is not of your making, and by securing a good deal you may in fact be helping them out as well. If you believe that dealing in these situations would weigh on your conscience, then bargain properties may not be ideal for you.

Bargain properties suit investors on low incomes and/or low equity, because they can help you to continue buying more investment properties in the future. If you have a low income it can be difficult to save the deposit for a rental property or fund any shortfall in rental income to cover expenses. If you have low equity, then banks are unlikely to continue lending you funds for more property until market forces have increased your equity situation sufficiently. Bargain properties allow low-income and/or low-equity investors a better chance of being able to continue buying further investment property.

Risk-averse investors actually suit buying bargain properties as they provide a buffer to adverse economic conditions such as falling house prices. Bargain properties often provide a good rental yield as well, which provides a buffer against factors such as interest rate rises. You do not have to wait for market conditions to increase the value of your property, as the value is already built in. In this way, bargain properties actually provide better security to investors than ordinary properties.

Investors with short investment timeframes suit bargain

properties because they accelerate you towards your goals on the day you buy them. Rather than waiting for market forces to increase the value of your property, you are acquiring the increased value. Some investors may have self-imposed short investment timeframes while others, such as older investors, may have short timeframes imposed upon them.

Overview of bargain buy properties

Advantages

- Extra equity is locked in from day one.
- Not reliant on an improving property market.
- Reduces your risk.
- Reach your goals faster.

Disadvantages

- Harder to find than ordinary property.
- You are often buying property at someone else's expense.
- There may be a good reason why it is cheap that you haven't discovered yet.

What investors suit a bargain buy property?

- Investors with the time to seek out bargains.
- Pragmatic investors.
- Investors with low equity.
- Investors with low incomes.
- Investors with short timeframes to achieve their goals.

Example of a bargain buy property

In this example, a property is bought for $170,000, 15% below true market value of $200,000. Six months after purchasing the property, it is revalued and the loan extended to $160,000, being 80% of the valuation. This reduces the required deposit to $10,000 and greatly increases the percentage return.

Property purchase price	$170,000
Deposit	$10,000
Rent (yield 8.3%)	$270 pw
Property manager at 7.5% of rental income and Interest Only loan	
Value of property after 10 years	$256,017
Equity after 10 years	37.5%
Return if sold after 10 years	$73,084
Excess rental income over 10 years	$6605
Cumulative annual return on investment	23.5% (average 39.7%)

Assumes 2.5% inflation rate; house and rental prices plus expenses increase by the inflation rate; mortgage interest rate of 7.5%; building depreciation clawed back; 50% of chattel depreciation clawed back; real estate agent fees.

Case study

A block of four three-bedroom flats on separate titles with large outside areas was on the market for $560,000. They were renting for between $190 and $220 per week, providing $810 per week total. Based on these facts, the property was on the market for a yield of around 7.5%. Both of the stairs that gave access to the top-storey flats were in poor condition and, although the property was fenced, the fence was unpainted and there was no landscaping, which put us off at first and probably put a lot of others off as well.

The vendors had another business opportunity they wanted to use the money for rather than keeping the flats. They were keen to move on to this new opportunity and the higher returns it could bring.

An investigation revealed that the rents being charged were well under market rates, which were $250 to $260 per week. This meant that the achievable rent was actually around $1000 per week or 25% higher than they were at present. Based on the achievable rent and other sales that had occurred, we estimated the value of the property to be around $620,000.

We offered $520,000 for the property with a one-week settlement after five days' due diligence on the property, with no other clauses. We hoped this would look attractive to the seller. Although the conditions looked attractive, the price didn't. However, after some negotiations we settled on $540,000 after agreeing to take on the existing tenants.

As expected, the valuation came in at $616,000, being around 14% higher than the purchase price. After settlement, we were able to increase the rent for two of the flats to $240 per week, an increase of $100 per week. By taking on the existing tenants, we were required to take them with their existing conditions. This meant we had to wait nearly six months before we could raise the rent on the other two units to $250 per week. Upon doing this, the weekly rental rose to $980 per week, which provided a 9.4% gross yield on the purchase price.

Martin Duncan
Mount Albert

7

Fixer-uppers

Properties in need of renovation (fixer-uppers or do-ups) have always been a popular option to create capital gains and improve your returns compared with ordinary property.

Properties needing attention are easy enough to find. However, many people think they are getting a bargain when, in fact, they are not. Given the state of the property, they are actually getting value for money, not a bargain. Many people buy a property then spend money doing it up, only to find that its market value is more or less the same as the original cost of the property plus the improvement expenses. This means that a lot of effort goes into creating something that you probably could have bought for the same amount of money, but for no effort.

As a general rule, do not spend one dollar on fixing up a property unless it will make you four or more in return. Although many people believe this is impossible, to allow for the risk of renovations going over budget plus a profit margin, you need to have this type of return. This means knowing what you are doing, planning in detail what renovations you will undertake and monitoring things carefully as you go.

When looking for a fixer-upper, it is essential to have a good idea of property prices in the area. If you are looking at a tired two-bedroom flat, you need to know what improvements you are going to do to the flat and, most importantly, what the flat will be worth when the improvements are completed. To do this, you need to have a good knowledge of two-bedroom flat sales in that particular area.

Often it is the investor's own time and physical effort that creates any added value in the property. Some say that if you paid yourself for your time then the improvements are not cost efficient; however, you could view the time spent as a second income for yourself.

A key point with fix-up properties is that there are risks involved with them and you need to be aware of the risks, make an allowance for them and build in a sufficient margin to cover for them, plus your time and a profit margin.

What to look for

Not all properties make good do-ups. Defective items that you cannot see generally do not add value to a property when they have been repaired or replaced. This includes such items as rewiring the electrics, replacing a hot-water cylinder, repairing mouldy or rotting weatherboards, flooring or roof joists. There are other factors that are usually too expensive to add real value to a property. These include re-roofing and altering the room layout. If you find a property that is poorly laid out, often with a mish-mash of rooms and a rabbit-warren feeling, it can be difficult to fix this in a cost-effective manner.

Kitchens and bathrooms need particular care when renovating. They are incredibly important to the value of the property and to tenants; however, they can soak up funds very quickly if not planned well. As with most investment-property renovations, cosmetic improvements are the best.

In the bathroom, new paint, floor coverings, toilet seat and bathroom accessories (shelves, cabinet, shower curtains, and so on) go a long way towards making the place look like new. A good-size mirror can help light a dim bathroom by reflecting available light, plus it gives the impression of space. A new bathroom vanity can also add value, although you may get away with new doors and/ or cabinet top. You should avoid replacing the shower as this is usually expensive and can involve new taps and expensive plumbing work as well. If you are replacing taps, do not skimp on price – the cheaper taps wear out fast and replacement parts can be notoriously difficult to find. Go for well-known brands and get the advice of your plumber rather than basing your decision on price and which style you like. Taps in rental properties need to be hard-wearing and reliable. Always add an extractor fan when renovating bathrooms, as they help to reduce mould and protect the property.

Kitchens should be approached in the same way as bathrooms. You want to try and avoid redesigning the layout. Make use of existing kitchen cupboards as much as possible. If you have to replace cabinetry, try and get a display or show kitchen from a kitchen manufacturer, rather than a custom-built one. Painting walls, putting in new cupboard doors and replacing bench tops can look fabulous. When replacing stoves and ovens, try and get good reconditioned ones, or else go for a reliable solid model from a recognised brand. Make sure elements are easily replaceable. A rental property kitchen should be functional, tough and easy to keep clean. Install an extractor fan to help protect the building's structure.

In general, cosmetic improvements are the kind that can add good value to a property. This includes painting walls, ceilings and architraves, replacing blinds and curtains (choose inexpensive ready-mades, or find curtains on special) plus carpet and other floor coverings. Carpet is not as expensive as it used to be, compared with other household items. The three items of painting, floor and window coverings cover virtually all inside surfaces of a property, so improving them adds a significant impact to the property and hence to its value. It is usually better to go for neutral shades as they appeal to a wider number of tenants, but avoid a bland look.

Good storage is always desirable, so if this is lacking in the property, try to add extra storage or install space-saver units within existing cupboards and wardrobes to make the best use of available space.

On the outside of the property, try and avoid large-scale items such as a new driveway, although painting the exterior can be good because it adds instant appeal as well as protecting your asset. However, the existing paint may be in reasonable condition and a wash may be all that is necessary.

Street appeal is important, even though you are not planning on selling the property, as it adds value and makes borrowing against the property easier. It also means that prospective tenants conducting a drive-by are more likely to want to see through the property. The front fence, letterbox, front door and front of the property are the usual factors combining to give good street appeal. These items need not be expensive to create a good impression and add value.

Regarding landscaping, pruning, thinning the plants and foliage and applying weed-mats with a suitable top cover such as bark or stones, can make the property look great and reduce maintenance issues. An outside area is highly desired by tenants and adds value to the property. This can be achieved with pavers or a deck for a reasonable cost. A basic pergola can help to link the building with the outside and finish the area off nicely.

Working out the details

If you have to cut corners and draw up a tight budget in order for fixer-up property to work on paper, it probably isn't a good deal to go for. It is better to allow for all the things that could go wrong and be slightly on the pessimistic side. Not too pessimistic, of course, or you will never buy anything. Make sure you consider how the work will affect your tax position, and prepare a detailed schedule of work and finance for the project.

Tax considerations

Timing of your renovations can have a bearing on your tax position. If you undertake work straight after purchasing the property, the IRD will judge that the cost of the renovations was capital expenditure and not an expense. This means that the cost of the renovation will be depreciated over the life of the items rather than written off in the year that they were made.

To claim renovations as expenses, the work must make good wear and tear caused by tenants. This would mean you couldn't undertake the repair straight after purchasing the property and claim it as an expense. Consider whether you want to wait a year or not. If you will be able to receive a higher rental price or revalue the property to increase your equity and make further borrowing easier, then you are probably better to conduct the renovations straight away. If the rental price is not going to be increased due to the renovations, or you don't need to use the increased equity the renovations will provide, or the renovations are not urgently required, then it may be better to wait.

Time

Time is of critical importance when undertaking renovations. It is very difficult to undertake major renovations yourself when you are completing them part time. It is also highly unlikely that you can rent the property and undertake major renovations, so there is an opportunity cost in undertaking them. That means that in addition to the cost of the renovations, there is the lost opportunity to collect rent. Every week that goes past is a week's lost rent.

You should calculate the time that it will realistically take you to complete the renovations yourself and factor in the lost rent over that period. It may work out that it will cost little more, or even be cheaper, to hire someone to do the work. Student Job Search can be a good supplier of reasonably priced and flexible labour.

Finance

After you have completed your renovations, the property should be worth considerably more. As you have undertaken activities to increase the value of the property, you can immediately get a re-valuation and apply to the bank for an extension to the loan. This could allow you to recover the cost of the renovation and also any deposit you used to purchase the property.

When you purchase a fixer-upper, you will likely have to pay for the renovations and it could take some time for a revaluation to be completed allowing you to refinance your mortgage based on the increase in value. If you do not have the necessary money to complete the task, a revolving credit account can be a good source of funds. You only take out what you need, when you need it, and are charged interest accordingly. As the funds are being used to provide rental accommodation, they are still tax deductible.

Advantages

The benefits of the fixer-upper are that you can add value to the property in a short timeframe. Like bargain properties, this increases your equity almost immediately and helps you to purchase further property. Unlike bargain properties, you should not have to wait for six months before being able to go to your bank and apply for an extended mortgage to account for the increase in value.

The increased equity allows a smaller cash investment, which in turn makes returns higher.

If you are handy and know what you are doing, you can help to reduce the cost of renovations and thereby increase your return. There are many different ways to renovate property and there is an opportunity to benefit from your past experiences, knowing what will and won't lead to a sufficient increase in value.

By undertaking repairs, you will provide better protection for your property, attract high-quality tenants and maximise your achievable rent.

Fixer-uppers are reasonably easy to find because many home-owners today have reduced the amount of maintenance they are undertaking on their properties and believe it is too much like hard work to undertake it when selling. In addition, many buyers lack the vision to see what could be accomplished with some clever use of renovation techniques, which reduces demand for this type of property.

Disadvantages

Whether you undertake the work yourself or pay others, fixer-uppers are going to be more work before and after you have completed the purchase.

Fixer-uppers are more difficult to find than ordinary properties and usually take more time and energy to get into a rentable state than bargain properties.

There is a risk that you have not investigated the property properly and surprises may undermine your renovation budget. In addition, there may be hidden problems that could not be identified until part way through the renovation. These cost overruns can evaporate any profit you were planning on and hinder your ability to borrow funds for further property purchases.

Investor match

Fixer-uppers ideally suit tradespeople or people with flair as a home handyman or decorator. If you need to employ tradespeople to do much of the work then it can become difficult, though certainly not impossible, to make a fixer-upper profitable.

Like bargain buyers, you need to have a lot of spare time to source these types of property as well as the time to fix them up, which can take weeks. DIYers are notoriously bad at estimating how long it will take to fix up properties.

Like bargain properties, fixer-uppers suit investors who have a low income and/or low equity or a short investment timeframe to achieve their goals. Like bargain properties, fixer-uppers offer the opportunity to pro-actively add value relatively quickly to an investment property.

Overview of fixer-upper properties

Advantages

- Opportunity to add value.
- Can seek extra borrowings once improvements are completed and added value confirmed.
- Often easier to find compared to bargain properties.
- Opportunity to conduct work yourself.
- Not reliant on an improving property market.
- Reduces your risk.
- Reach your goals faster.

Disadvantages

- Harder to find compared to ordinary properties.
- Big time commitment to fix up before able to be rented.
- Risk of cost overruns and unexpected additional repairs.

What investors suit a fixer-upper property?

- Tradespeople or home handyman.
- Investors with sufficient time to find the right properties and fix them up.
- Investors on a modest income.
- Investors with low equity.
- Investors with a short timeframe before retirement.

Example of a fixer-upper property

In this example, a property is bought for $165,000, with $7000 spent on renovating it, increasing its value by $35,000 to $200,000. When renovations are completed the property is revalued and the loan extended from $137,600 to $160,000, being 80% of valuation. This extension of $28,000 reduces the initial cash requirement of $34,400 (20% of purchase price plus $7000 for renovations) to $12,000.

Purchase property	$165,000
Deposit/investment after revaluation	$12,000
Renovation cost	$7000
Value after renovation	$200,000
Rent (yield 8.2%)	$270 pw
Property manager at 7.5% of rental income and Interest Only loan	
Value of property after 10 years	$256,017
Equity after 10 years	37.5%
Return if sold after 10 years	$73,084
Excess rental income over 10 years	$6605
Cumulative annual return on investment	21.5% (average 33.1%)

Assumes 2.5% inflation rate; renovation adds value by a factor of 5; house and rental prices plus expenses increase by the inflation rate; mortgage interest rate of 7.5%; building depreciation clawed back; 50% of chattel depreciation clawed back; real estate agent fees.

8

Developments

Developments differ from fixer-uppers in that you are adding to the property or developing the property so that it is different from before. By developing a property, you are maximising the return that you can achieve from that property.

When we think of developers, we usually think of people who build houses and earn a living by on-selling them. However, in this strategy we are not planning on selling, but on keeping them as rental properties.

The strategy is to enhance the properties in some way that goes beyond merely making what is already there more attractive or returning it to its previous condition. This is how they differ from fixer-uppers.

There are a wide range of developments that can be applied to rental property, from changing the use of the property, to subdividing a multi-unit site and building new dwellings.

A simple change of use development or dividing a large bedroom or lounge to create an extra bedroom does not require a high degree of knowledge or expertise. But adding extra dwellings or subdividing can be very involved and have unexpected problems and costs. These types of developments are unlikely to suit new investors or those without practical knowledge of the process.

With a varying level of risk, it is advisable for investors to build in a healthy profit margin so that if the development does not go to plan, then at least a small profit is made and a loss or indeed a forced sale is avoided.

Types of developments

The following are some examples of the type of developments you can undertake.

Changing the use of the property

One of the easiest and less risky ways to develop a property, changing the use of the property usually involves little cost and effort. An example is purchasing an ordinary home near a learning institution and adapting it for students. The increasing number of language schools is altering this market dramatically. An ordinary four-bedroom home previously let to a family may have been bought for $200,000 and rented for $300 per week, providing a 7.5% return plus capital gains. By providing a fridge, washing machine and clothes drier, plus some other furniture, you make it easier for students to occupy the property. Students can pay $100 to $140 per week each for a suitable property, increasing your rental return to between 10% and 14%, after spending $2000 on whiteware and furniture. Other features to add could be extra phone lines into bedrooms so tenants can have individual Internet accounts if they want to.

When changing the use of a property, be careful to identify if there are extra regulations that may apply after your development. As an example, adding extra rooms could turn the property into a boarding house. This would change the regulations that the property would be operated on (note that at the time of writing a major change to the Residential Tenancies Act was going through parliament that would see boarding houses brought under the RTA. See www.PropertyInvestor.Info for updates). Fire regulations would also change which could mean hardwired fire alarms need to be installed and numbers placed on bedroom doors.

Another option to change the use of a property is to fit it out for use by the disabled. The disabled can have a difficult time locating homes that meet their needs and tend to be excellent, long-term tenants when their needs are met. The cost of making your dwelling suitable for disabled tenants can also be offset through government grants.

Adding a room

The biggest determinant of rental income and property value is the number of rooms a property has. By adding a room you can increase the achievable rent by between 25% and 100%, depending on the number of rooms available before your development, plus gain a good capital appreciation. This can make adding a room a very worthwhile undertaking. The options for adding a room include creating an extra room from within the existing floor plan, extending the property or adding a sleepout.

Dividing a large room is often the easiest method of adding an extra room to your property. L-shaped or large lounges or large bedrooms provide the easiest opportunities to achieve an extra room; however, in older properties, large laundries or a combination of laundries and entranceways could be utilised. Resource consent or a building permit are usually not required for this type of work, which helps to make the undertaking even easier.

Converting an L-shaped lounge can simply be a matter of

having a non load-bearing wall and a door installed. If feasible, it is better to position the new bedroom door so it opens out into the hall. There may already be an existing door into that part of the lounge, which will make the additional room easier to create. Note the position of lights and light switches, as these may need to be installed or altered for the space to be used as a bedroom. This is usually straightforward; however, the extra cost should be budgeted for.

A bigger problem can be windows. If there is no existing window or the window extends across the new wall's location, then extra work will be needed. This can start to eliminate any gain you might make from the development; however, it is usually not a prohibitive undertaking. Take care to price the work well and be sure of the increased value and achievable rental price.

Creating two rooms from one is similar to converting the lounge, although there can sometimes be problems with access doors. If the existing door is in a poor position, it can either be boarded up and two new doors installed, or a mini-entranceway can be created where the existing door is, allowing two new doors to be installed, giving access to the rooms.

Case study

I have found that the only way of moving towards my property goals is to use strategies that increase the rent and equity on every deal I do. This way, not only is my equity going up immediately but also the rent covers expenses, so it is not what I call a 'crocodile' (you always have to feed it so it doesn't turn and bite you!).

I recently went to view a property in Hamilton that had been on the market for over six months. It was on the market for $144,000 and that was a reduced price. As a three-bedroom Hamilton home on a small site it was expensive. The lounge had a dogleg, which to me was an obvious opportunity to convert into a fourth bedroom.

It just so happened that a young guy who had just joined the Waikato Property Investors Association was at the house viewing it at the same time as me. I thought I would show him the potential of the property and pointed out to him how it could be converted to a four-bedroom house very easily. It would give him extra rent of up to $80.00 per week and increase the value of the property by about $30,000.

He didn't take my advice, so I bought it myself for $136,000 and upon completing the wall, which I built with a double wardrobe and soundproof gib costing under $2000, it valued up at $170,500 and currently rents for $300 per week (which is now under the current four-bedroom Hamilton rental market of $320 per week) as the tenants stayed on from the previous year.

Another property I purchased in Meadowbank, Auckland, for $160,000 was a one-bedroom unit with an extra-big lounge. I divided the lounge with a cavity slider for a cost of about $2000 and turned this room into a second bedroom. This room has no windows, which is why I chose a cavity slider, so it could open right up and let the light in.

As a one-bedroom it was getting $220 per week rent, and now as a two-bedroom I am getting $310 per week. The bathroom is off the original bedroom, but most people who have rented it are couples, who still want an extra room to use as an office.

To achieve this exceptional rent I have also installed a fridge/freezer, washing machine and drier, and rent it partially furnished with two couches, a coffee table, vacuum cleaner and dehumidifier (all the furniture is second-hand).

The cost of the furniture and alterations has been returned in the first year. The cost of altering the layout and semi-furnishing the property was approximately equal to the increased rent for one year.

I have had quite a few tenants from overseas, who have just arrived in the country and need somewhere to live while they look around for something to purchase. I have also rented it to overseas students who do not want to buy a lot of furniture.

By simply adding extra rooms, the rent goes up quite considerably and so does the property value. This way I can 100% finance the next deal, even when I borrow the money for adding the walls.

Some people think tenants are attracted to big living areas, but reality is, if they live with other people in a flatting situation, they quite often like to retreat to their own bedrooms for privacy and watching TV, so they only need room for a couch and dining-room table in the living area.

I look for property that has a big lounge, as this is the easiest way to add another room and especially if the wall just needs to go straight across the middle of the room.

Anita Milroy
Auckland

Adding a bedroom by extending the house is a more expensive exercise. However, you are increasing the floor size of the dwelling without the extra costs of kitchens and possibly bathrooms, activities that tend to increase the per metre cost of a development. When adding a room, care should be taken that it fits well into the existing layout, both externally and internally, as a 'tacked-on' bedroom can look so bad it actually devalues the property.

Even though it is more expensive to build a room like this, the extra rent often makes it warranted. If the room costs $20,000 to build and generates an extra $100 per week in rent, this is a 26% return on your investment and should increase the overall value of the property.

A sleepout is another option for adding a room or rooms to a property. A sleepout will need a suitable base-floor and roof. However, it does not need to physically or aesthetically match the main dwelling as much as an extension does. The main dwelling does not need to be altered to accommodate the sleepout, which can make it more cost effective to build. Compared with an extension, it is relatively easy to build a two-bedroom sleepout rather than just one bedroom. Naturally, this can further extend your return.

Because a sleepout is not considered as valuable as a bedroom incorporated into the main dwelling, it will not increase the value or rental price of the property to the same extent.

Garages can be converted into sleepouts relatively easily, as they already have walls, floor, roof and electricity supplied. Care should be taken to ensure that they meet health and safety regulations before being let, especially check that the concrete does not let in moisture. When completed properly, a converted garage can provide a very cost-effective sleepout.

Note that resource and building consent will usually be required for an addition such as a sleepout and almost certainly for an extension. You should consider aspects such as site coverage and angles from boundaries in your plans. Regarding building plans, after 1 July 2003, councils can apply Resource Management Act issues to building consents, which could see the cost of many developments increase. See www.PropertyInvestor.Info for updates.

Building a minor dwelling

A minor dwelling is a small unit, typically under 65 square metres, which can be added to a property without the need to subdivide or cross-lease the section. A 65-square metre dwelling is actually quite large, allowing for two or even three bedrooms and therefore a large increase in rent. A minor dwelling can make excellent use of a large section because the return in rent is only from the cost of the unit, not the land. This raises the average return for the property as a whole.

Not all councils within New Zealand allow minor dwellings and some have different rules on what they will allow. Because of this, it is always advisable to contact your local council to establish if you can build a minor dwelling and what rules you will have to follow. Like all other constructions over one metre, minor dwellings fall within the Resource Management Act as well. This will mean considering aspects such as site cover, trees, car parking and turning circles. Usually, these will not be an issue because the new dwelling will be relatively small and will not be pushing the boundaries of what is or isn't acceptable.

Although constructing a minor dwelling sounds a lot easier than building a new house, it is still a separate habitat, requiring its own separate services. Often, the most expensive will be water services and drainage. However, drainage can usually be incorporated into the existing structure, which makes the process easier than a completely separate structure on its own section.

Buying and moving a minor dwelling can be a profitable exercise (moving a house is covered in the following section). Minor dwellings can be found in newspaper classifieds and publications such as *Trade and Exchange* and *Loot*. This can be a very cost- and time-effective option compared with building a structure from scratch.

Another option is to convert a sleepout or garage into a minor dwelling. If converting a garage, as with sleepouts, care should be taken to ensure that the base will not allow moisture to enter the dwelling as this can be extremely unhealthy, and would not pass health and safety regulations. Landlords have faced fines in the tens of thousands of dollars for providing unhygienic accommodation to tenants.

Be aware that many new subdivisions may have covenants that prevent minor dwellings even if the local authority allows them.

Moving a house

There are many reasons why a house is no longer required at a particular location. It may be because the values of properties in an area make it unfeasible to renovate the house, the owner wants to use the land for another building, the design no longer fits with the area, or by removing it the section can be further developed with multiple dwellings. Whatever the reason, one person's rubbish is another's treasure. However, moving a house is a huge undertaking that should not be undertaken lightly or ill prepared.

It is usually far cheaper to move a house onto a site and renovate it, than it is to build a similar house from scratch. However, there are a number of similarities. They are both large projects, you will need land to put the house on, you will need to use a lawyer, a building consent is required, you need to fit within the Resource Management Act, you will need to connect services, landscape the section, and gain a code of compliance certificate on completion.

To be sure that the project you are going to undertake is financially feasible, research what similar properties to the building you propose to move into the area are valued at. Things can and do go wrong when moving a house, so you should have a healthy profit margin to provide you with security. Construct a budget for the project under the main headings of land, house purchase, moving costs, renovation and landscaping. It is essential to allocate an amount for unforeseen items under each of the main headings, as it is almost a certainty that something will be forgotten or there will be cost overruns.

Although it is better to have a property where you can subdivide the land to place your movable house, buying a section is also an option that can prove profitable. An aspect you should be wary of is covenants on the section, which may exclude movable dwellings. Another aspect is finance. Lenders usually require a higher equity level when purchasing a section on its own, so you will either require sufficient equity in another property, including your home, or a large cash deposit. Once the development is completed, you should be able to refinance with better terms.

Your local council may also have restrictions on moving houses, so check with them as well. Easements are another potential problem to eliminate. An easement is a legal right registered against the section. This could be for an item like a stormwater drain that runs through your property. An easement could be placed on the section so that you cannot build over the drain or the council has the right to dig it up should it require repairs.

Drains can be the bane of developers' lives, whether moving a building or constructing a new one. Particular areas have problems with drainage and it is worth knocking on the door of neighbours to identify any potential problems. Getting a Land Information

Memorandum (LIM) is another good way of finding potentially negative information about a section.

If the new section is sloping, it will cost more to re-site the house on it. If the slope is severe then poles will need to be sunk very deep to stop the house from slipping away. This can add to the cost dramatically, leading to expensive drilling as well as the increased cost of the poles. It is amazing how much earth needs to be removed for large poles to be inserted, and the expense of the truckloads it takes to remove it. Get some indication of costs from the house removal company before looking at sections and get them to inspect the site and quote before going unconditional.

Access is another consideration, although it is incredible where removal companies can take a house. Of course, the more the removal company has to do and the harder the job is, the more it will cost you.

Houses for removal are located in newspaper 'For Sale' classifieds, or in papers such as *Trade and Exchange* or *Loot*. Removal companies have yards full of houses and it is a bit like going to a shop to buy one. They also have dwellings that they can move straight from their old site to your new site. This can be advantageous, as it involves one shift rather than two and places less strain on the dwelling.

Buildings come in many shapes, sizes and conditions. Make sure you thoroughly check the house so you know it is what you want and can predict how much it will cost to renovate. Always budget for things costing more than you think because invariably things go wrong or you miss certain items that need repairs, such as rotten support timber. A preliminary costing is a good idea as it will quickly tell you if this property is right for you before wasting time getting quotes, and so on.

You will likely spend a lot of time dealing with the council and obtaining a building consent and will need items such as floor plans, elevations, site plans, drainage and pile plans to get approval. It is possible to do a lot of this yourself with help from the removal company and a surveyor.

The removal company pretty much handles everything to do with the move. It detaches the dwelling from its existing piles, lifts it, takes it to the new site and repositions it on new piles. Once the house is in place, you organise for the services to be attached and begin renovating.

The whole process can take a few months, so detailed planning is essential to keep the project on track and reduce the length of time you are incurring expenses without any income.

For further information, see Hans Doevendans's book, *House Removals in New Zealand* (published by Lowlands Publishing, PO Box 2487, Hastings).

Subdividing and creating another section

Subdividing a section can be an excellent way to create increased equity in a property. A dwelling on a half-site is likely to achieve a similar rental income as the same house on a full site, so subdividing is unlikely to have a large impact on your rental income. Likewise, the combined value of a subdivided section and the house on the remainder of the section is greater than the value of the house on the previous large section. So subdividing creates extra value. By subdividing a rental property you are unlikely to lose any rental income and the reduced value of the remaining property will be less than the value of the section. This provides the opportunity to sell the section to reduce your mortgage, thereby increasing your equity and income.

Cross-leasing used to be a favourite method of splitting a property, as the rules for cross-leasing were less restrictive than for a full subdivision. There are problems with cross-leases, however. Under a cross-lease title, all cross-lease holders own the land in an undivided share and contract to each other the right to defined areas for dwellings, driveways and exclusive areas. On the title, these areas are clearly marked out, including the dwelling. Any addition to the building or the construction of a garage or shed needs the approval of the other cross-lease owners and a change to the cross-lease plan. If this isn't done, then problems can arise when selling the property. The many problems and confusion that cross-lease properties have caused have led to a decline in their popularity. Councils tend to offer the same guidelines for cross-leases and subdivisions, so the benefits of cross-leasing really do not apply any more.

If you believe that a property is subdividable, it is a good idea to confirm this by employing a land surveyor before going unconditional. Even if the property is large enough to be subdivided under zoning allowances, it may not be practical to do so because of the position of the existing dwelling, which, for example, may be positioned in the middle of the existing section or may not allow sufficient access to the proposed new section. These problems can be overcome by moving the dwelling to a new position on the section; however, this incurs extra costs that must be accounted for.

Assuming the section is subdividable, you would need to employ a land surveyor to investigate the site and prepare a site survey plan that shows the existing section levels, dwelling, paths, driveways, trees and services. The surveyor will also prepare a report detailing how the development complies with the Resource Management

Act and local council rules. Both reports are then lodged with the council for approval. Even if the proposal does not comply with the rules, the council may still give approval if the non-compliant areas are considered minor and have little or no environmental effects.

In addition to application fees, the council will also charge a reserve contribution, which is intended to cover the costs of developing existing and new parks within the area. These reserve contributions can be high, so it is advisable to get an idea of the cost prior to purchasing the property or undertaking other expensive items in the subdivision process. By calling the local council they will be able to explain how the reserve contribution is calculated. The means of calculation is generally set down in the council's District Plan.

Once the subdivision is approved and all works completed and signed off by the council, a surveyor will produce land transfer plans, which will show the new boundaries and means of pegging them. These plans are then lodged with Land Information New Zealand (LINZ) for examination and approval.

Once the subdivision receives LINZ approval, all the paperwork is provided to your lawyer, to complete the necessary conveyancing work. As the subdivision in this case would involve an existing dwelling, approval of the mortgage-holder would also have to be obtained, as it has a registered interest over the property.

Taxation is an issue with this type of development, as anything other than a minor project could be considered a development, and any capital gains could be taxable. There may also be GST issues. It would be advisable to discuss the matter with your accountant or tax advisor.

Subdividing and building a new rental unit

Subdividing and building a new rental unit can be an excellent method of increasing a return on a property, as you gain two rental incomes without having to pay the full cost of two properties. This can generate increased equity plus a higher average yield over the two or more properties that you will have at the end of the project.

Naturally this strategy will be more involved and take longer to complete.

Advantages

The obvious benefit of developing a property is that you can create an immediate capital gain and increase in rental income. Like bargain and fix-up properties, this gives you added protection against a downturn in the property or rental market, makes it easier to acquire further investment property, and moves you towards your goals at a faster rate than ordinary properties.

When planned and executed well, developing properties can bring enormous returns to an investor and can turn an ordinary investment into an excellent one.

Because many people fail to see the development opportunity of particular properties, such properties can be easier to locate and buy. This can save time in the purchase phase of the investment.

Disadvantages

Depending on the scale of the development, there is a high level of risk. Many things can go wrong when developing a property, especially when subdividing and building a new dwelling. Factors that can undermine a development include unknown costs such as drainage, electricity supply and other services, plus resource consent, reserve contributions and complying with other council regulations. If you have only planned on a 10% profit margin and cost overruns amount to 10% or more, then you are in trouble.

The time commitment for just managing a large project is high, especially when you are inexperienced and/or maintaining a full-time job. Developments can take a long time to complete, meaning no income is available, yet costs such as mortgage payments must still be met. This can lead to cashflow problems or high holding costs eating into profits if the project takes longer to complete than first envisioned.

Estimating the value of a development once completed can be difficult and it may pay to contact your land surveyor who can give estimates for these development costs. In some cases, projects that have gone to plan cost-wise can still provide little or no return.

If you sell part of your development to help fund the remainder, there could be tax issues and the risk of tainting. *(Tainting is where your property developments taint your property investments, so the IRD treats them in the same way as your developments, leading to capital gain tax implications.)* It is essential to take good tax advice from a professional who is well versed in property matters before you take this option.

Investor match

Developments ideally suit tradespeople or professionals such as draughtsmen, architects, surveyors or from other professions involved in the building industry.

Developments can be small in nature, however they usually require a high level of involvement. Because of this, development properties require investors to have a lot of spare time to source these types of property as well as managing the development, which can often take months. Due to the timeframe of many development projects, investors who can take lengthy breaks from work or business can suit this type of strategy.

Like bargain properties and fixer-uppers, developments suit investors who have a low income and/or low equity or a short investment timeframe to achieve their goals. Developments offer the opportunity to pro-actively add significant value to an investment property and really accelerate you towards your goals. While developments can increase equity quickly, there may be a requirement for working capital with larger projects which make them difficult for investors with limited equity, requiring them to start with smaller projects and build themselves up.

Larger developments are very involved projects and suit well-organised people who are comfortable with things going wrong, problem solving and accepting that there is a relatively high level of risk compared to other investment strategies.

Overview of development properties

Advantages

- Opportunity to add significant levels of value.
- Possibility of conducting some of the work yourself.
- Not reliant on an improving property market.
- Reduces your risk once completed successfully.
- Reach your goals faster.

Disadvantages

- Harder to find than ordinary properties and fixer-uppers.
- Often a big time commitment in the development phase.
- Risk of being classed a developer and tainting other investment properties you own.
- High risk of cost overruns and unexpected occurrences depending on degree of complexity.

What investors suit a development property?

- Investors with time to undertake such projects.
- Investors with some experience in building, either through a trade or profession.
- People with large holiday breaks or other forms of down time.
- Investors with good equity but little time to achieve their investment goals.
- Young investors who want to build up an equity base quickly.
- People with good project management experience.

As there are many ways to develop property it is difficult to provide an example that is representative of the different options. Instead I present three further case studies of investors who have undertaken rental property development.

Case study 1

We had a property in Palmerston North that we bought in 1992. It was actually two 1200 square metre sections side by side. We relocated three older houses onto one section, leaving the other section sitting idle for a few years until we built up more equity.

Over the Christmas student break we relocated another large five-bedroom house onto the spare section. The house had to be cut in half to be moved and we found that by setting the house down with a two-metre gap between the two halves, we could achieve a bigger lounge and still be just within our section coverage. It was a simple matter of filling the space in between, giving us a better living area. Doing away with the original front entry also created another bedroom. We changed the bathroom/laundry area to give two toilets, one in the bathroom and another one off the laundry. We also fitted two separate showers, both with extractor fanlights, which vent to the outside. These fans run for about seven minutes after the light is turned out and clear a lot of moisture from the air. We repainted the whole of the inside one colour, with the doors one shade darker. All bedroom doors have deadlocks to give the student tenants added security.

The cost of the project was $23,500 to relocate the house to the section and place it on piles, plus a little under $30,000 to renovate. The house is now rented to students at $70 per room per week generating $420 a week in rent. We rent the house for a fixed period from 1 December to 30 November the following year, and provide the first 10 weeks at half rent. This gives us $19,740 a year in rent or around a 37% return on the cost of the development.

Ron Dudson
Palmerston North

Case study 2

In 1989 my wife and I purchased a property in the South Auckland suburb of Papatoetoe, for $90,000. It consisted of a four-bedroom, 1960s-style weatherboard house, with a separate single garage on a rectangular-shaped, quarter-acre (about 0.1 hectare) section. The rental was $240 per week, providing a 13.9% return.

The following year we decided to build on the rear of the property. We looked at many different low- to medium-cost new home companies, but couldn't find anything that really stacked up financially or tied in with the older established homes in the neighbourhood. We then looked at second-hand relocated houses. Having researched the costs of building new, it soon became apparent that the right second-hand house was a far cheaper option, especially as we planned to live in the house for a short time and undertake any renovations ourselves.

We ended up purchasing a three-bedroom home from Glenfield, built in the early 1970s and still being lived in. The house was quite similar to our existing house, but had the added benefit of having recently been fully renovated, including a new kitchen and bathroom and new carpet throughout. The house was being moved to make way for extensions to the neighbouring retirement home.

We paid $39,000 for the house (plus $500 for the separate single garage), which included re-siting onto footings, ready for connecting to services, and basically moving in.

As the house was relatively small, it was moved in one piece without the need for cutting to transport and arrived with no damage at all. All up, including consent fees, service connections, site developments (shifting existing garage and paths, and so on), setting the building on its new site, redecoration, etc, we spent a total of $67,000.

On completion the new relocated house had a rental value of approximately $210 per week, which provided a healthy 16.3% return on our investment – and combined with the $240 on the front house gave us an overall return of 14.9% for the property.

Following the success of this project, we have since relocated a further three houses. Two were houses on properties we owned, where the houses were located towards the centre of the sections, prohibiting further development. By moving them to the rear of the sections, we were able to get a further two and three more sections (respectively) to build on.

While moving a house can be rewarding if you get it right, I wouldn't suggest it's everyone's cup of tea and we certainly heard of (and saw) a few nightmares along the way. People had simply either chosen the wrong house for their site or had underestimated the amount of work that can be involved in relocating an older house.

Nigel Smith
Auckland

Case study 3

Our criteria for undertaking a project is that its total cost must be paid back through increased rental prices in no more than five to seven years. We had a three-bedroom property, which we bought for $112,000 and were renting for $180 per week to students.

By extending the rear of the property, we were able to convert it into five bedrooms. We did this by incorporating a laundry and outside toilet into a bedroom, plus using the existing lounge as a bedroom. The existing kitchen, bathroom and toilet were pulled down and the back of the house was rebuilt and extended to provide a new kitchen, laundry and toilet, plus a good-sized living area.

To better accommodate students, we had telephone cabling and extra power sockets installed in each bedroom and the new lounge and put locks on the bedroom doors. All keys for the bedroom doors would also operate the main entrance door.

The property was renovated, including gibbing the four front rooms (although I now use 9 mm MDF instead of gib). The entire interior of the property was painted and carpeted.

After development and refurbishment, we were able to charge $75 per room, increasing the rent from $180 to $375 per week, or around $10,000 a year. The total cost of the development, including loss of rent, was around $25,000. This meant that the payback period was well within my criteria.

The total cost of the property, including the original purchase and development, was $137,000, but it was valued at $225,000 on completion, a capital gain of $88,000. This increase in value meant that my equity in the property was nearly 40%, more than enough for the bank to be happy for it to stand alone.

Cliff Seque
Dunedin

9

Pay Off Debt

This strategy focuses on owning a predetermined number of mortgage-free properties by your targeted retirement date. You start by establishing how many properties you will need to buy and how you will pay them off by the date you intend to live off the income.

The number of properties you will require is estimated by taking the income you desire, adding 30% to cover running costs such as rates and insurance, then dividing this by the annual rent you should receive from the type of property you intend to purchase.

Assume you wanted an annual income of around $45,000 at retirement and are intending to buy properties for around $200,000, yielding a minimum of 10% or $385 per week. Your calculation for determining the number of properties you require would be:

Desired income	$45,000
+ 30% for expenses	$13,500
Equals	$58,500
Divided by annual rent	$20,000
Equals	2.93

In this example, you would need to purchase three properties to achieve an income of around $45,000 before tax. Assuming you borrowed the entire $600,000 at an average interest rate of 7.5%, then it would take you around 25 years to pay off the mortgage using excess rental income. You could speed this up by paying a deposit to reduce the initial size of the mortgage or using your own money to pay off the debt faster.

This is a lower-risk strategy as it does not involve high exposure to any potential downturns in the housing market, there is a lower level of borrowing and it is relatively easy to plan. However, it does not make use of leverage to the same extent as other strategies, which means that it can be comparatively slower to reach your goals. But it is better than saving all the money and then buying the property, as you are locking in the purchase price in today's dollars and can use increasing rental income to pay off the loan. Investors using this strategy need to have a good income stream, a good deposit or a high rental-income property, or a combination of all these factors for this strategy to work effectively.

Principal repayments are usually slow over the first few years, then speed up as you have compounding income to apply against the debt. To allow greater flexibility, at least some of your debt should be in a revolving credit account or floating facility so you can make extra payments as and when possible.

Tax planning is essential, as after a few years you will start to make a profit due to the size of the mortgage reducing. Only the mortgage interest portions of the loan repayments are claimable as a tax deduction. This means that over time some of the rental income you receive will need to go towards paying income tax.

To maximise income, it is a good idea to buy high-yielding and low-maintenance property, conduct the property management yourself and do as much of the maintenance as you can.

You can also make good use of tax refunds obtained through depreciation claims to help reduce your debt.

Advantages

The key benefit of this strategy is surety. As there are fewer factors involved in the strategy, there is less to go wrong, less effort on your part, less exposure to risk and it is easier to map out your plan.

Because you are paying off the loan on the property, you are less exposed to future interest rate rises. As the size of the loan is reducing, your equity is also increasing, thus reducing your exposure to a downturn in the property market.

If the market remains flat or goes down, you will be less affected as you have increased your equity by paying off debt.

If you do not have much free time, this strategy does not involve as much time hunting for lots of property deals and managing properties.

If you are a cautious person, you will feel better knowing that the debt is being reduced.

If you plan to keep the property or properties, depreciation clawback is not an issue for you. (It is an issue for the beneficiaries of your estate, however, and good legal advice should be sought to minimise the potential impact of depreciation clawback.)

Disadvantages

The biggest downside is that the strategy does not take full advantage of leverage. As you are only buying the number of properties that will provide your required income, you are not using the increasing value of extra properties to help you along.

Because you are not using the accelerating benefits of leveraging, it is likely to take you longer to reach your property goals. As you are not as involved in the market, it can also feel like a slow strategy. You don't get the buzz that some people feel when they are out in the market looking for and buying property.

This strategy is not as tax efficient as other strategies, because paying off debt means that you will be paying income tax earlier.

Although you do not need to spend as much time looking for more property, in order to make the few properties you do purchase cashflow positive, you will need to spend time either searching for bargains, fixer-uppers or developments or have a high income, or both.

If you do not buy high-yielding property, you may need to invest your own money, either up-front in a large deposit or with regular top-ups, to ensure the loan is paid off in the timeframe you have set.

If you put in a large deposit to ensure an average yielding property provides sufficient cashflow to meet your goals, your return on the investment is lower.

Investor match

As this is a slower strategy compared to other property strategies, paying off the loan tends to suit investors with a long timeframe to reach their goals.

Paying off the loan means you won't need to buy so many properties, compared to other strategies, and your debt levels will not be as high. This factor means that risk-averse investors may suit this type of strategy or new investors who are getting a feel for the industry and how it operates.

Investors who do not have a lot of time to look for and manage property suit this strategy. It may take them longer to find the right property, however they do not need so many properties and have the time to be patient.

Loans are paid off faster when the initial borrowing is low or extra funds can be used to accelerate repayments. Consequently investors with a high cash reserve to invest in property or high incomes are ideally suited to this type of strategy, as they will reach their goal faster than others who are not in the same financial position.

Overview of pay off debt properties

Advantages

- Lower-risk investment option.
- Less exposure to increases in interest rates.
- Pro-actively increasing equity through debt repayment.
- Low time commitment compared to other strategies.

Disadvantages

- Doesn't take full advantage of leverage.
- Longer timeframe to reach your goals.
- Not as tax efficient as other strategies.
- Requires some effort to pay off the loan.

What investors suit a pay off debt property?

- Young investors with a long timeframe to reach their goals.
- Investors who are risk averse and patient.

- Investors without much spare time.
- Investors with high incomes.
- Investors with high cash reserves to invest.

Example of a pay off debt property

In this example, the rental yield is higher than in the examples for previous strategies.

Purchase property	$200,000
Deposit	$40,000
Rent (yield 10%)	$385 pw
No property manager and property paid off in 18 years	
Value of property after 10 years	$256,017
Equity after 10 years	62%
Return if sold after 10 years	$135,707
Excess rental income over 10 years	–$3204
Cumulative annual return on investment	11.8% (average 23.1%)

Assumes 2.5% inflation rate; rental prices and expenses increase by the inflation rate; mortgage interest rate of 7.5%; all income from property and extra capital applied against the loan; building depreciation clawed back; 50% of chattel depreciation clawed back; real estate agent fees.

10

Borrow and Never Pay Off

This is a strategy that confuses many people, as the thought of never paying off the loan leads them to believe you can't make an income from the property. The strategy is based around buying high-yielding property, similar to the type used for paying off the loan, but instead of using the excess income to pay off debt, it is used for your own personal income.

To calculate how many properties you will need, you divide your desired annual income by the excess cashflow of the property you are targeting. For instance, if you bought a $200,000 property with a rental yield of 10%, borrowing the entire $200,000 at 7.5%, then you could have a positive cashflow of around $2900 a year after expenses and tax, including depreciation claims. If your goal is to have an income of $30,000 after tax, then you would need around 10 of these properties to achieve your goal.

Structuring your finance becomes critical, as rising interest rates have a big effect on your income. In the above example, if your interest rate moved just over two percentage points higher, to 9.65%, you would lose your income from the property entirely. Long-term fixed rates would provide more certainty.

You would also need a high level of equity: to purchase

10 properties without deposits, you would need equity from another source, most likely your home, of at least $400,000, plus sufficient equity for your home as well to maintain an overall 20% equity position.

If you have sufficient excess funds, however, you do not need to totally finance all the investment properties. That way, you would increase your income through lower interest payments and reduce your exposure to interest rate fluctuations. Using the above example but with a $15,000 deposit per property, the annual income would be $700 a year higher, at around $3600. This means you would need eight instead of 10 properties and your borrowings would be $1,480,000 instead of $2,000,000.

While this strategy is never to pay off the loan, you can still retire debt as the values of the properties increase. Using the above example of purchasing 10 properties, each time prices rise by 10% you effectively own one of the properties mortgage free. You could sell it and retire debt, which has the effect of reducing your debt levels and maintaining your income through reduced interest payments on the remaining properties. Of course you can sell property at any stage, not just when you effectively freehold one.

Under this strategy, you would be purchasing property with the possibility of never selling – just living off the income. If the properties never go up in value, then there is still the possibility of depreciation clawback when you die and your beneficiaries inherit the properties. This is because depreciation assumes that the buildings are going down in value to their written-down book value, not the price you paid for them. In this way, even if the buildings' market value has stayed the same, depreciation clawback will still apply. With no increase in the value of the properties, your beneficiaries are actually inheriting a liability in the depreciation clawback. Assuming a reasonably long retirement, it is more likely that the properties will have gone up in value, however.

Given that depreciation clawback is likely to be an issue for the beneficiaries of your estate, it is likely that you would want to take steps to avoid the problem. One option is to purchase the properties through a loss-attributing qualifying company (LAQC; see page 146) and bequeath the shares in the property company to your beneficiaries. By doing this, the shares in the company, not the property itself, transfer to the beneficiaries. It is only when the property is disposed of (i.e. has a new owner) that depreciation clawback is triggered.

Even if you do leave a liability, it is a liability with a good cashflow and the beneficiaries could choose to implement the 'pay off the loan' strategy to increase the equity.

A further point on bequeathing investment property is that in order to be able to claim depreciation you need to have actually paid for the asset. If you inherit a property, it has no cost to you; therefore there is nothing to depreciate. If you inherit the shares to a property company, then the property has not changed hands and the company can still make depreciation claims.

Advantages

The benefit of never paying off the loan is that your cashflow is established from day one. By living off the income, you get an instant income increase with each purchase, rather than having to wait for loans to be paid off or values to increase, which would allow you to sell some property and reduce debt.

Because of the speed in generating an income, you can reach your desired income goal in a few years rather than a few decades.

Disadvantages

You are highly exposed to interest rate increases that could easily see your income eliminated entirely. Worse still, your rental income could become insufficient to cover your expenses. This could lead to a mortgagee sale situation.

In order to purchase the required number of properties to meet your income goals, you will need a high level of equity to obtain the loans.

In order to receive a sufficient income level, it is likely you will need to own a large number of properties and will have to self-manage them through your retirement to maximise income. The more properties, the greater the management effort.

If you are pushing your equity limits, a fall in the property market could see your equity reduced to a point where the bank wants you to sell property to improve the situation. Hence timing the market could be critical.

If the property market doesn't increase before you die, you could be leaving a liability to the beneficiaries of your estate (even if it is an income-producing liability).

Investor match

Never paying off the loan suits investors with a short timeframe, such as a few years, in which to reach their goals. Often this will include older investors approaching retirement.

As the strategy requires a high level of equity to work, it suits investors who have a high-value, mortgage-free home that they can use as security for the loans necessary to purchase the required number of investment properties.

By never paying off the loan there is a high risk of being caught out at some stage with rising interest rates. For this reason investors who are comfortable with taking risks are more suited to this type of strategy, and long-term fixed interest rates are advisable.

Overview of borrow and never pay off properties

Advantages

- Cashflow established from day one.
- Ability to quickly reach your income goals.

Disadvantages

- High level of borrowings.
- Highly exposed to interest rate increases.
- High level of equity required.

What investors suit a borrow and never pay off property?

- Older investors or investors with a short timeframe to reach their goals.
- Investors with high equity in their home but a low income.
- Investors who are risk takers.

Example of a borrow and never pay off property

Purchase property	$200,000
Deposit	$0
Rent (yield 10%)	$385 pw
No property manager and Interest Only loan	
Value of property after 10 years	$256,017
Equity after 10 years	37.5%
Return if sold after 10 years	$33,084
Excess rental income over 10 years	$37,871
First-year rental income	$2898
Cumulative annual return on investment	infinite as no money in

10 of these properties equals a $28,980 per annum income after tax

Assumes 2.5% inflation rate; rental prices and expenses increase by the inflation rate; mortgage interest rate of 7.5%; all income from property taken as drawings or income; building depreciation clawed back; 50% of chattel depreciation clawed back; real estate agent fees.

11

One Size Does Not Fit All

In order to explain them simply, discussions of the six strategies presented in chapters 5 to 10 have focused on each of the strategies independently. In the real world, however, there is often an overlap of strategies within a single property purchase. Deciding on one particular strategy does not preclude you from switching to another strategy as circumstances change. In fact, your long-term goal may be accomplished through planned moves from one strategy to another as you progress.

When looking for property, you may find a bargain opportunity for a fix-up dwelling where you can develop the back section. Remember that it is not a bargain simply because you can add value to it. It is only a bargain if you could turn around and sell it again straight away for more than it cost you to purchase – making you one step ahead from the beginning.

To be a fixer-upper, it needs to be in such a condition that you could fix it up and increase the value of the property by at least *four* times the renovation costs.

A development opportunity must stack up on its own, after allowing for the bargain price and extra value of fixing up the existing dwelling. For example, will the combined value of the original dwelling on a smaller section plus the newly created section be worth more than the cost of the development?

The bargain is a given and will give you more confidence to undertake the fix-up and development. However, both these activities have inherent risks, which mean they must work individually. The desired return on investment is your choice as an investor.

There are many combinations of strategies that you could undertake. For instance, you may decide to purchase a high-yielding property with the aim of paying off the debt over time. However, you may find a property that fits with your plan and also provides the opportunity to add a minor dwelling that increases the yield so the loan can be paid off at a faster rate. Why would you not take such an opportunity? In fact, you can plan to incorporate different strategies from the beginning.

Your strategy could be to purchase bargain properties that may also be fixed up for extra profits, or high-yielding properties that have development opportunities – or any other combination of options that work for you. The point is that there are many ways to invest in property, and you need to consider the best way for you at this particular point in time.

Be aware, however, that the more conditions you put on an investment property, the harder it will be to find. This could mean you need to be realistic about how many of these properties you will be able to purchase over any particular timeframe.

When you are considering different strategies, remember that the appropriateness of the strategy can change over time. You may undertake a high-risk, high-effort strategy when you are young, then change to a lower-risk strategy once you have established a certain level of equity or income from your properties and no longer want to risk what you have achieved. For instance, you could use your home as security for buying investment property and maintain a 20% overall equity level and neutral cashflow position until you have bought, say, six investment properties. You are, arguably, undertaking a relatively high-risk strategy, pushing your equity and cashflow boundaries. At a predetermined point in your plan, you may sell one or two properties to reduce your borrowings and increase your cashflow, then change your strategy to repaying debt and buying cashflow-positive properties while maintaining, say, a 30% equity level. In this case, the plan is to move away from a higher-risk strategy towards one that offers lower risk in order to provide better protection for the gains you have made. The third stage of your plan could be to stop paying off debt after a particular period of time, maintain your debt levels and start living off the rental income your properties provide.

The point is that you are in control of what you do, how you do it and when. This is one of the beauties of investment property. However, with this control comes a level of responsibility. If you make all the decisions, even if it is in consultation with a property coach or other investors, then it is you who must 'carry the can' if it all goes wrong. This is where proper planning is critical. The next chapter shows you how to put everything together to form a personalised plan that will work for you.

12

Putting It All Together

Throughout this book we have looked at why you should set goals for your property investments and how to base these goals on the income you want to achieve from property. We have considered your personal and financial circumstances and the six strategies that can be employed to invest in property. In this chapter, all this information is put together in order to prepare a written plan that will meet your desired goals – and, at the same time, take regard of your present financial and personal circumstances, your strengths and weaknesses and your approach to investment risk and reward.

Choosing a strategy

Although it is sometimes blindingly obvious which road you should take towards reaching your property investment goals, this is not always the case.

Sometimes you may not have the knowledge needed to undertake the strategies that seem right. If this is the case, then this challenge needs to be overcome through either self-improvement and acquiring the knowledge yourself, or employing others to carry out either all or some of the tasks necessary to undertake the strategies.

Acquiring the necessary knowledge can involve attending seminars, courses or night classes, reading books and magazines, going to university or employing a property coach. I'm a great believer in all property investors joining their local property investors association (see page 150 for contact details), as this is an excellent way to pick up on a wide variety of knowledge that can be unobtainable in any other way.

You may decide that it is better to employ the services of others to help you overcome obstacles in undertaking specific types of strategies. This may include a wide variety of tradespeople, consultants, property finders and other professionals.

By up-skilling yourself or employing the services of others, it may be that you can undertake strategies that otherwise wouldn't be open to you. The most important point is to consider all the various factors detailed in this book and to choose the strategy or combination of strategies that best fits you, your situation and your goals. Do not be concerned if this takes some time – it is worth getting right. The more you want the goal and develop a sound strategy to achieve it, the more likely you will attain the goal. You then have the desire and belief that you can do it.

When you have decided how you are going to attain your investment goals, you can now work out how many properties you will need to own. This can be a test of whether the goal is realistic or whether you need to work out a different strategy that makes the goal realistic.

To work out how many properties you will need to own, you need to identify the approximate net rental income you are likely to receive from that property type when it is debt free (assuming you are not undertaking the 'never pay off the debt' strategy) and any planned improvements have been completed. To do this, estimate the annual income in rent, then take away all the estimated costs, including maintenance, and an allowance for rental down time. This will provide you with the net rental income per property. It is then a simple matter of dividing your income goal with this figure to estimate how many debt-free properties are required.

Total rental income – total expenses
= net rental income per property

The following example assumes the investor's goal is to buy property for $156,000 with a minimum 10% rental yield.

	$
Total rental income	15,600
Rates	1300
Insurance	250
Maintenance	450
Allowance for down time	600
Property manager	1170
Total expenses	3770
Net rental income	11,830

The target number of properties then becomes: income goal divided by net rental income per property. So if your income goal is $35,000 before tax, the equation to determine the number of properties required would be:

$$\$35{,}000 \div \$11{,}830 = 2.96$$

The before-tax income figure is used because it is diffcult to estimate what depreciation allowances and tax rates will be in the future.

By multiplying the target number of properties by their individual value, you will establish the total value of properties that you will require to provide you with your income goal.

$$3 \times \$156{,}000 = \$468{,}000$$

With this information you can better define your goal. An example could be: by X date I will have a before-tax income of $35,000 from three mortgage-free properties worth a total of $468,000 in today's value, yielding a 10% gross rental return and being professionally managed.

You will then need to look at how you are going to acquire these properties freehold and if you can do so realistically.

Your strategy could be to buy bargain properties at, say, a 10% discount on fair market value, using $10,000 you have saved as a deposit and applying any excess rental income against the mortgage, then selling down at a predetermined point to enable three of the properties to be mortgage free. Assuming an average 2.5% capital growth rate, you could achieve this goal by buying one of these properties each year for 12 years, then selling nine of them in order to be mortgage free on the remaining three. (Remember to be cautious when estimating expected capital gains. If capital gains are higher than you have allowed for, then you will reach your goal faster than expected.)

If this was within your timeframe, comfort zone and appeared realistic, it would form the basis of your strategy. This is just an example. It is certainly not the only strategy that would achieve the same result, so do not assume it is the best answer for the given example. Remember that there are many ways to invest in property and what is right for you may not be right for someone else.

Whatever your strategy, do the numbers and work out what you have to do to achieve your goal. This can take some time – however, it is well worth the effort.

'What if' scenarios

Once you have established a suitable strategy – but before committing yourself – it is wise to consider potential negative events or factors that may have an impact on your investment strategy.

The big three are: non-existent or negative capital gains, reducing rental prices, and increasing interest rates.

If you consider the negatives before making a purchase, then should they occur they are more an inconvenience than a threat to your investment – and you will be less likely to panic and sell the property prematurely.

Lower than expected capital gains

When the property market is rising or has been high for quite some time, it is easy to expect that these rises will continue and plan for them in your strategy. However, this is exactly when it is more likely that prices will stabilise or fall rather than continue to rise. If you base your property plan around expectations for high capital gains, then it is likely that on paper any old property will give you a healthy return and look like it will work. This may lead you to purchase the wrong type of property.

Lower than expected capital gains are unlikely to bust you; however, they can slow you down from achieving your goals.

Negative capital gains are another story. If your strategy is to purchase many properties over a short period with the expectation of an upwardly rising property market creating equity to permit further purchases, then you could be in for a shock. Property markets work in cycles, so there is a chance that the market will turn against you, particularly in the short term.

With this in mind, work out how your strategy would work if prices fell by, say, 10% rather than rose. How close would you be towards pushing the equity boundaries and making the mortgage-holders nervous? If this exercise shows that you could be forced to sell one or more properties, then you may wish to reconsider your strategy. If it would merely slow you down, then the risk may be worth taking given the information you are working from.

Reducing rental prices

Rental prices are not based on your costs but on tenant demand and, to a lesser extent, the supply of rental property. Tenant demand can change quite quickly, even if the overall population remains the same or even increases. If the economy falters and employment becomes unstable, many tenants may take measures to cut their costs. As housing is usually a large component of their overall expenditure, it is likely to be one of the first expenditure items to be looked at.

Tenants may look for cheaper properties to rent or move to cheaper rental areas. Although this does have a negative effect on the higher-priced rental properties and areas, it tends not to reduce rental prices greatly as there is a corresponding increase in demand for cheaper properties and locations.

What often happens when tenants reduce expenditure is that there is an increase in the number of people per dwelling. For instance, a couple in a two-bedroom property may take in a boarder rather than have a spare bedroom. Another couple may move from a two-bedroom to a one-bedroom property. A family may move from a three-bedroom property to a two-bedroom one and have children share a room. Students or younger people entering the workforce may stay at home rather than move into a flat. When these changes become widespread, they can quickly have a negative effect on the demand for rental property and lead to reducing rental prices.

Unlike commercial property, however, where a lack of demand can lead to long periods without a tenant, residential rents usually fall by about $20 or $30 a week. If you accept this change in market conditions and lower your rental price, it is more than likely you will get tenants. However, many new investors plan for rental increases and if these don't occur, or rental prices fall for a period of time, they cannot afford to keep the property.

For this reason it is a good idea for each new property purchase to establish how you would be placed financially if rental prices decreased. If it would slow you down but not break you, then you should not be at risk of being forced to sell the property. If it means you could not afford to keep the property, then you may want to take another look at the risk you are taking and come up either with a different strategy or a contingency plan.

Higher interest rates

Mortgage interest payments usually make up a large proportion of total expenses for a property investment; therefore, an increase in interest rates often has a large and negative effect on cashflow and your ability to hold on to a rental property. This becomes increasingly relevant as the number of properties you own increases, along with your borrowings. This is why it is critical to examine the impact of interest rates rising by at least two percentage points (say, from 7% to 9%) and evaluate the impact of such an outcome.

For every $100,000 borrowed, a 1% rise in interest rates adds almost $20 a week ($1000 a year) to your costs. If you have borrowed $2 million, then a 1% increase adds around $400 a week ($20,000 a year) to your costs, and a 2% increase would add $800 a week ($40,000 a year) to your costs.

Fixed interest rates provide a buffer against rising interest rates, and even if they are higher than floating rates, they may reduce your exposure to interest rate rises.

Triple whammy

It is not unknown for all three of these negative occurrences to happen at once. This happened in many New Zealand markets over the years around 1998 to 2000 and forced many over-extended investors to sell some or all of their properties.

Although this was difficult for those investors, it provided some excellent buying opportunities for others who had placed themselves in a better position. It goes without saying that you are better off being in the buying camp. However, none of those who were forced to sell planned to be in that position. In all likelihood, they failed to plan at all. This is not to suggest that you should try to predict the market and stop buying if you think it is overheated. It just means be aware that it could happen and you should buy property that reduces your risk exposure should it occur.

Once again, work through an exercise to establish what would be the result on your property investments if a triple whammy occurred soon after you made your purchase.

Write down your plan

Once you have determined your goal and conceived a strategy (or combination of strategies) for accomplishing it, you should write it down. Committing your plan to paper makes it real, clarifies your thinking and makes the plan easier to follow and complete successfully. You do not need to show the plan to others if you do not wish to – and often it is better not to. This is because some of the people you confide in may not believe the plan is achievable and put you off, or they may have their own ideas and distract you or try to convince you that their way is the right way. There are many paths to achieve success in property so be sure of what you are doing and stick to it.

Your plan should contain your goal, which should be specific and follow the SMART principle described in chapter 2. Next, you should include your current financial position with a breakdown of your assets and liabilities (to show your current net worth) and an income statement. Your financial position should be updated annually or whenever you make a property purchase or some other significant change occurs to your financial situation.

Under your plan, you should analyse yourself, including the time you will devote to investing in property. Time is a large consideration in how active you are going to be and the likelihood of finding the type of deals you hope to. If you have little time to spend on finding property, it is unlikely you will have the time to find bargain properties or work on fixer-uppers.

It is a good idea to state the number of days and hours you are going to spend working on your investments. This means thinking about and defining the best times to read newspaper classifieds and property-specific advertising, contact your agents, hand out fliers, analyse options and view property. When you have a few properties, you will need to allocate some time on their management (although some of this will be reactive. While writing this section I have had to organise an electrician to fix a power problem with a property).

Following your goal, financial statement and self-analysis is a detailed description of the strategy you will undertake to achieve your goal. This should include information such as the type of property you are going to purchase or develop, the location, approximate value, yield, and the number of properties you aim to purchase and when.

You should write down how you plan to fund your investments, including the amount of equity you want to maintain before making subsequent purchases, whether you will add value to accumulate the equity, whether you will use your own savings as a deposit or to pay off debt, or whether you will use excess rental cashflows. You need to write down how you will operate your cashflow, whether there will be excess funds or whether you will top up the rental income with your own funds.

If you have a loan on your home, your plan should include how you will pay it off or transfer the personal debt to tax-deductible rental property debt. Having a home mortgage means that you should have interest-only mortgages on your investment properties, at least until your home mortgage is eliminated.

Your plan should include any major future events, such as going overseas for an extended period, getting married, having children, starting a business, upgrading your home, extra studies or career development. These events can have an impact on your time, income or expenses, or all three, which in turn could affect your property investment.

How the investments are owned – in what type of structure – should be included in your plan. It is best to consult a professional tax and legal advisor, or at least a property coach, before deciding on which structure to use (see chapter 13).

For further reading on structures, see Mark Withers's book, *Property Tax in New Zealand* (available for $24.95 from Withers Tsang & Co Ltd, www.wt.co.nz).

Establishing rules

When purchasing investment property to meet your goals, it is essential to set rules – establish boundaries – about what you will and will not consider. These rules could involve yield, capital gain and location. By setting and sticking to rules, you not only have a better chance of attaining your goals, it also saves time in searching for property and you tend to become more specialised in what you are looking for.

When specifying yield returns, these should be stated taking any planned improvements into account. For example, if you had a 10% yield rule and a fixer-up strategy, you would not pass up a 7% yielding property if you could undertake some form of improvement that would reach or surpass the 10% yield. In this example, you could refine your rule further – to purchase property yielding at least 7% with the potential to improve and attain a 10% yield. Another rule could be that the section you buy has to be subdividable or capable of housing a second minor dwelling or be within two kilometres of a learning institution. Whatever the conditions are that fit with your strategy, write them down.

Note any obstacles

It is likely that you will need extra knowledge to achieve your intended strategy. Identify any obstacles or challenges that you will need to overcome and whether you will seek the knowledge to overcome the obstacle yourself or employ someone else to do it. If you are going to seek the knowledge yourself, write down what it is you need to learn and what course, study, books, websites, government department or council will be able to provide this knowledge. Include the team that you will need to undertake your plan, including agents, lawyer, valuers, accountant, mortgage broker, tradespeople etc and have a system so that their names and contact details are easy to find. Build good business relationships with them to ensure loyalty and good service.

With all this information in one place and written down, you now have a comprehensive blueprint of how you are going to attain your goal. By writing it all down, it is real and far easier to follow. It is also measurable, so that you can go back to it and ensure you are on track.

It is not set in stone, however. If the plan needs modification then make the changes necessary to correct whatever isn't working and get you back on track to attain your goal.

Goals and strategies – checklist

The following is a list of questions and factors you should consider when developing your property plan. You may not choose to provide answers to all these questions; however, you should at least consider if they are appropriate for you and your plan. These items can form the headings for your property plan.

Background information

1. Why am I investing in property?

Goals

1. When do I want to receive a passive income from property?
2. What is my passive-income-from-property goal?

Financial situation

1. What are my current assets and liabilities?
2. What is my net worth?
3. What equity level do I want to maintain when buying property? 20%, 30% ...?
4. What is my current income from working?
5. What is my current passive income?
6. What is my current monthly expenditure?
7. What are my budgeted monthly savings?

Self-analysis

1. What major personal events are likely to occur that will impact on my investments?
2. What are my strengths and weaknesses?
3. What is my attitude towards risk?
4. How much time can I commit to investment property?

Strategy

1. What strategy will I use to achieve my property goal?
2. What locations am I going to specialise in?
3. What type of property am I going to invest in?
4. How much income will this property generate?
5. What expenses, excluding mortgage payments, will this property have?

6. How much income will this property generate per year when mortgage free?
7. How many properties will I need to obtain my passive-income-from-property goal?
8. How many properties will I need to purchase each year to reach my goals?
9. How will I maintain sufficient equity in my property to reach the target number of properties I need to acquire?
10. How will I maintain sufficient cashflow to reach the target number of properties I need to acquire?
11. What are the consequences of a two percentage points increase in interest rates and rental price falls of 20%?
12. What will I do, if anything, to minimise the risk of interest rate rises and rental price falls?

13

Implementation

Putting things in place

Once you have your goal and strategy established, there are some steps to take before you actually make your first purchase. The first is to discuss your plan with an experienced investor, property coach or property investment professional, with the aim of checking the feasibility of your ideas and establishing aspects you may not have considered. This could lead to identifying problems you hadn't considered or receiving tips to make your investments easier. Other items to get in place are your ownership structure, finance and investment team.

Ownership structure

You should consider the structure you will use to own your rental property at an early stage as you could incur extra costs if this is undertaken later. Which structure is right for you and your personal situation needs to be considered carefully, and it is advisable to get professional help from a property expert, accountant, lawyer or all three. Accountants tend to look at structures from a tax point of view and lawyers from an asset protection point of view. For this reason, it may be advisable to hear comments from both parties before deciding on which structure or combination of structures you will use. Keep both professionals involved and aware of what each has suggested.

Owning property in your own name or in partnership is the simplest and cheapest option; however, it is also the least flexible in terms of allocating income and profits, plus it offers no asset protection.

Trusts are primarily for asset protection; however, they can be useful if the property is producing an income and the investor is in the highest income tax bracket. This is because trusts are taxed at a flat 33% rather than the higher 39% personal income tax rate. The usual downside of trusts is that losses cannot be used to reduce an investor's personal income tax in the year the losses are made. Losses in a trust are accumulated until the properties are in a profit-making position and can then be utilised.

An increasingly popular structure for owning property is the loss-attributing qualifying company (LAQC). These are companies that have been granted 'loss-attributing qualifying' status by the IRD. This offers you flexibility and limited protection, plus allowing the owner or owners to access any tax losses the company makes in the year they are made, which is great for cashflow. A second key benefit is that investment property capital gains can be distributed to the investor as a tax-exempt dividend. This can also be an excellent method for converting personal debt to tax-deductible debt. For example, say your investment property rose in value by $50,000 and you had a $50,000 mortgage on your own home. You could raise a $50,000 loan through your LAQC, pay it to yourself as a dividend from the capital reserve and use the funds to pay off your home mortgage. You have effectively transferred $50,000 worth of debt from being non tax-deductible to being tax deductible. Even if this means you need to use your own money to maintain your rental property cashflow, you are still better off by doing this. If you have not set up the LAQC before purchasing your rental property, you may need to sell the property into the LAQC at a later stage, which will incur extra legal fees and probably depreciation clawback.

Remember that a company isn't an LAQC until it has filed an election form to join the regime. You can establish a LAQC yourself. (If you do so, always follow up any verbal communication with the IRD with a confirmation letter, email or fax. If anything does go wrong you will then have a paper trail to use which can save you time, money and a lot of hassles.) However, it is probably advisable to get an experienced person to do so, such as your accountant or lawyer. Although the process doesn't take long, for reasons stated earlier, it is better to sort this out before buying property rather than after. Trusts are more complicated and can take longer to establish. If necessary, shares in the LAQC can be transferred to the trust, which negates selling the actual property to the trust.

Finance

If you are using mortgage brokers to obtain finance, then take your plan to them so they can see your situation and where you are going. Taking note of your plan, they should be able to provide expert advice on which type of mortgage is right for you and arrange to get pre-approval for finance.

Pre-approval is actually not the guarantee of finance that people think it is. However, it is usually a good indication of what you can borrow, and your mortgage broker will let you know whether or not it is a realistic amount for your circumstances and fits with your plans. You can also use a due diligence clause in the sale and purchase agreement, which will cover finance should a problem occur.

Another advantage with pre-approval is that your paperwork should be more or less completed and ready before you require it. This can save both time and hassle, when time is at a premium and hassles are everywhere. Having your affairs in order can make investing a lot more pleasurable.

Your team

Establish all the trade and professional services you are going to need as part of your property team, and seek out those who are experienced in rental property and whom you trust and could work with. Keep all their contact details in a central place so they are easy to find and access.

At the very least, your team will consist of an accountant, lawyer, mortgage broker, some real estate and buyers' agents, valuer, insurance agent and associated tradespeople. In addition, you may wish to employ a property coach who can help you develop your plan and offer independent advice and help along the way, plus act as a confidential sounding board who isn't personally involved but has expertise in property.

Another consideration is a property manager. If you are uncertain about your ability or desire to manage the properties yourself, then at least plan to employ a property manager. In this way you will have already allocated the cost, which will make the decision whether or not to use a manager easier in the future.

Other members of your team will depend on the strategy you have adopted. They could include a builder, surveyor, architect and draughtsperson.

It is wise to have thought about the team you will require at an early stage so you can seek recommendations from others and know that you are getting experts in their field.

Perhaps the best part of your team should be all the members of your local property investors association. This is an ideal way to meet potential members of your team or at least get good recommendations for who should be on it. In addition to networking with other property investors, these associations provide excellent local knowledge and good speakers to keep you up to date with what is going on in the industry. In association with the New Zealand Property Investors Federation, associations also lobby local and central government and act as a voice for all property investors in New Zealand. They are not-for-profit organisations which provide extremely good value for money to investors and cannot come recommended highly enough.

Tools to help you

Property investors associations

There are sixteen property investors associations around New Zealand. They operate in a non-profit capacity and provide a wonderful resource to local landlords. Most are affiliated to the national body, the New Zealand Property Investors Federation. The main functions of these associations are to provide independent information to investors, a forum for meeting other investors to share ideas and knowledge, and a political voice for all New Zealand property investors.

Different associations provide different resources to members; however, all provide great value. All property investors should be members of their local association. Contact details follow on the next two pages. More information and resources are at the NZPIF website at www.nzpif.org.nz.

New Zealand Property Investors Federation
PO Box 13373, Johnsonville, Wellington
Ph: 04-477 5055. Fax: 04-477 5049
Email: nzpif@premiercall.co.nz
Website: www.nzpif.org.nz

Northland
PO Box 1640, Whangarei
Ph: 09-438 3322

Auckland
PO Box 10104, Auckland
Ph: 09-379 9692
Fax: 09-815 8641
Admin@APIA.org.nz

Waikato
PO Box 4346, Hamilton
Ph: 07-858 0799

Rotorua
91 Old Taupo Rd, Rotorua
Ph: 07-573 8464

Tauranga
PO Box 5345, Mt Maunganui
Ph: 07-575 9337

Gisborne
PO Box 707, Gisborne
Ph: 06-868 6357

Hawke's Bay
PO Box 1143, Napier
Ph: 06-835 1082

Taranaki
PO Box 94, New Plymouth
Ph: 06-758 8966

Manawatu
PO Box 6000, Palmerston North
Ph: 06-354 9969

Wellington
PO Box 1831, Wellington
Ph: 04-472 9877
Fax: 04-383 8950
wnpia@clear.net.nz

Nelson
PO Box 198, Nelson
Ph: 03-544 4019

Canterbury
PO Box 4396, Christchurch
Ph: 03-366 5978
www.cpia.co.nz

South Canterbury
152 Le Cren St, Timaru
Ph: 03-688 0690

North Otago
166 Thames St, Oamaru
Ph: 03-434 8275

Otago
PO Box 6051, Dunedin
Ph: 03-476 6400

Southland
PO Box 5121, Invercargill
Ph: 03-217 4479

PROPERTY COACHING

Property coaching can speed up your investment property knowledge so you feel more confident about what you are doing and avoid many of the mistakes that new and ill-informed investors unintentionally make.

Clients include new investors; investors with one or two properties who are looking to advance their investments; investors who have many properties but require feedback on structures, taxation and the appropriateness of the properties they own. Property coaches should provide independent advice to their clients and often become a confidential sounding board to examine property plans and individual purchases.

Benefits of using a property coach

- ✓ Examines your personal and financial situation and offers frank feedback on what you can realistically achieve through property.
- ✓ Examines the appropriateness of different investment strategies.
- ✓ Tax-deductible fees (including clients who don't have an investment property, but buy one in the same tax year!).
- ✓ Develops sound property plans that take account of your personal and financial situation.
- ✓ Discusses which areas are best for you to invest in.
- ✓ Ensures that any purchase works with your plan and doesn't hinder reaching your investment goals.
- ✓ Reveals changes you may need to make in your life to achieve the goals you have set.
- ✓ Establishes buying rules to follow.
- ✓ Analyses deals you are looking at.
- ✓ Answers questions about areas of investment property that you are unsure of or how they relate to your personal circumstances.
- ✓ Helps maintain your focus on achieving what you set out to do.
- ✓ Avoids the common mistakes other investors make.
- ✓ Develops an expert team to help you succeed.
- ✓ Gains confidence in what you are doing.

Andrew King – Property Coach

Andrew King has helped many people to make their investment in property a success.

You will gain access to years of experience within the industry that enables Andrew to quickly establish your circumstances and provide advice and information that will help you to gain what you want from property.

Andrew is not involved in either selling or finding property deals for clients, so he is impartial about how you can find property deals, the appropriate number of properties you should buy and timeframes you should stick to. He charges a reasonable hourly rate, with no up-front fees or minimum charges. You only pay for the services that you both require and feel you are getting value for.

Comments from clients

'When I began investing in property I read a lot of books and attended a variety of seminars. These were great but very generic. I really didn't know where to start ... What yield should I aim for? Should I buy units or a house? Where should I buy? etc. My first coaching session with Andrew answered these key questions and filled in the missing pieces of the puzzle. This gave me the confidence to get under way and within a month I had signed up my first property. Andrew was there for support during this process answering questions as they arose. I think our first investment is a good one based on sound criteria carefully worked out with Andrew.' *A. Stevens, Point Chevalier*

'A very BIG thanks ... being conservative in nature so I had to get my head around the whole thing before feeling comfortable. When it finally came to signing the dotted line, I was amazed how relaxed and unemotional I was!' *Kaye (& Wayne) Bird, Torbay*

For more information on Andrew's coaching services, seminars and other products and services to help you with your property investments, visit his website at

www.PropertyInvestor.Info
email Andrew@PropertyInvestor.Info
Phone 09-815 8642
Fax 09-815 8648

Acknowledgements

Although there have been many people who have helped to develop my knowledge of property over the years, I would like to personally thank four experts in their fields for directly assisting me to complete this book:

Sue Tierney, Director of Mortgages by Design, and 2003 Mortgage Broker of the Year

Glenn Metcalf, Registered Surveyor of Barry Satchell Consultants

Tony Steindle, Director of Steindle Williams Legal, and specialist property lawyer

Mark Withers, Director of Withers Tsang and Co, and author of *Property Tax in New Zealand*

Thanks also to the investors who shared their stories within this book, and helped other investors in the process.

I would also like to acknowledge all the wonderful people I have met through the property investor associations around the country and especially in Auckland.

Sincere gratitude goes to all my friends, new and old, who have helped me with their advice, wisdom, expertise and criticism when I needed it. Thank you all.

Special thanks to my family, especially my sisters, who are just wonderful people adding many colourful aspects to my life.

Most appreciation of all goes to my lovely wife Sarah, who has put up with many late nights of work, listened to my thoughts and encouraged me to action.

About the Author

Andrew King has had a love of property since childhood, saving for and purchasing his first investment property by the age of 24. He has always managed his own properties and enjoys this aspect of being a property investor. His passion for the industry led him to developing the *Auckland Landlord* newsletter in 1996, which provided current and independent information to Auckland Property Investors. The newsletter grew into the national magazine, *Residential Property Investor.*

Andrew has been a committee member of the Auckland Property Investors Association since 1998, and has been the president of the association since 2000. He has spoken at property investment seminars and written for several magazines and newspapers, including the *New Zealand Herald* and *Sunday Star Times.* He has appeared on the television programme *Money Matters* and is often sought by radio stations and other media to share his knowledge on property investment matters.

Andrew is the co-author of the bestselling book *The Complete Guide to Residential Property Investment in New Zealand,* which has been referred to as 'The Bible' for New Zealand property investors and has become an essential reference tool for many readers.

Andrew is still an avid property investor who also provides his knowledge on rental property as a property coach for property investors.